CW01614574

I WANT A CAMPERVAN

THINGS YOU NEED TO KNOW BEFORE BUYING (OR CONVERTING) A CAMPERVAN

SUMMER BOURNE

Printed in the United Kingdom

First Printing, 2019

ISBN 978-1-9999009-1-5

Dream-it Publishing, Wiltshire, UK

Front Cover photo by Aurelien at Unsplash

Blog and website: www.thecampercookie.com

Other Books by Summer Bourne:

'The Camper Cookie: Easy Recipes and Cool Tips for Your Campervan Life'

'Adventures of a Lazy Campervan Cook'

Disclaimer

This book is presented solely for educational and entertainment purposes. The author and publisher are not offering it as professional services advice. While best efforts have been used in preparing this book, the author and publisher make no representations or warranties of any kind and assume no liabilities of any kind with respect to the accuracy or completeness of the contents and specifically disclaim any implied warranties of merchantability or fitness of use for a particular purpose. Neither the author nor the publisher shall be held liable or responsible to any person or entity with respect to any loss or incidental or consequential damages caused, or alleged to have been caused, directly or indirectly, by the information contained herein. Every situation is different, and the advice and strategies contained herein may not be suitable for your situation. You should seek the services of a competent professional before beginning any purchase.

Contents

1. So, you want a campervan...

Well, as you are reading this book, I guess that you have decided that you can't live any longer without owning a campervan, hey, I totally understand!

I am always excited when we throw some clothes and food in the back of our campervan and head off into the wilds for an adventure. And even in the winter, when we aren't vanning much, it is fun to plan the trips we will have in the summer. When you own a campervan, your year becomes a series of wonderful holidays to look forward to and you get to regularly relax and re-charge in a way that makes life stresses seem less important.

You Want to Get it Right

But how do you find the best campervan for YOU? It is an expensive purchase and you want to get it right which can be hard to do if you haven't been campervanning or even tent camping before. You need to know what to look for before you choose a van. And everyone is different: a family with young kids will be looking for something very different to a twenty something surf dude or a retired couple.

You may even decide that you want to convert your own van so that it will be exactly the style and layout that you really want. Either way, I believe, you need to get very clear about who you are as a camper, what your priorities are, what the options are and what can realistically be achieved on your budget. So, I have put together this little book on how to choose or design a campervan and the questions you need to ask yourself before you do.

Don't Forget to Make it Fun

I am not a professional converter or the world's leading expert on campervans, and this is certainly not a technical book on owning a campervan or converting a panel van into a camper. However, we have been camping for many years, owned a micro-camper and have now converted our own van (a Vauxhall Vivaro called 'Big Red') which involved hundreds of hours of research. These are the sort of questions I wish we had asked ourselves before we bought our first camper and definitely before starting a conversion. Also, if there is more than one person who is going to use the campervan, you want to make sure that you are both/all thinking the same way before you hand over the cash. So, hopefully, this book will give you a good starting point for some interesting discussions but don't forget to make the process fun, too.

Campervanning is a wonderful way to explore, relax and get out in nature which I think is so important in this crazy, digital age that we now live in. I hope that *'I Want a Campervan'* will help you find the best campervan for you and your co-travellers so that you will experience the deep joy that is to be had from '*living the dream*'.

Happy Vanning!

Summer

2. What sort of camper are you?

Virtually everyone I talk to about our campervan adventures seems to have a secret yearning for a campervan themselves. We all want to be 'Living the Dream' and why not? But many people assume that this has to stay just a dream for them because it's beyond their lifestyle or budget. However, I believe, it really is possible to find a campervan that is affordable and that will easily fit in to your life as long as you don't need to have anything enormous or one of the super-deluxe versions. There is a campervan for YOU out there somewhere.

Glyn and I got our first camper, 'Trev-the-Prev' (a converted Toyota Previa) back in 2014 and we had some great adventures in him (check out my website www.thecampercookie.com for some pics). At the time, although we had been tent-camping for many years, we had never really thought about getting our own campervan as we just assumed that it was something beyond our reach. Looking back, it's strange that we thought that way because we hadn't actually done any research or really looked in to it, we had just made an uninformed assumption (or as my friend Liz calls it - an arse-umption!). This wasn't helped by the fact that when we started to look around the camping shows we found that most of the campervans were £30,000 plus and we would have only been able to scrape together maybe a tenth of that. At the time, Glyn was still financially supporting his first family, so it didn't leave a lot of cash spare for buying a campervan.

Determined to Get a Campervan

However, as time went on, we became more determined to get a campervan one way or another as we fell totally in love with campervanning after we hired one of those big, white motorhomes on a Groupon and spent a magical week touring Cornwall (sorry, I wasn't a campervan geek then so I can't remember which model it was). As it was a Groupon, they hadn't given us one of their newest vehicles and it did rattle alarmingly as we drove down the motorway, but we had a wonderful week in the West Country exploring ancient sites and beautiful landscapes.

We knew we had to get a camper vehicle of some kind, but we also knew that we wanted something smaller. Taking the motorhome down the tiny, high-hedged lanes in Cornwall had been a bit tricky and it had even restricted our adventures at times (can't be having that!).We also had to get used to being glared at when we were trying to park in a supermarket car park!

But we simply couldn't afford any of the cute VWs or similar vans. Then I came across a company on an internet search called Bumble Campers who hire out and sell converted Toyota Previas for under £5,000. We wanted to try one first, so we rented one of their vehicles for a weekend and found that it was a great little camper. To cut a long story short, we eventually found a Previa base vehicle for around £1,000 and Bumble were able to convert it for us so that the whole campervan had cost under £3,000! Obviously, being in a vehicle of this size does have its limitations but Trev-the-Prev gave us our first step on the campervan ladder.

Goodbye to Trev, Hello Red

Trev had been a cool dude but we knew it was time to let him go to his next person (a man in Scotland who camps in Trev on his historical re-enactment weekends) and we decided that we wanted to convert our next van ourselves. Our couple of years camping in Trev had shown us what was important to us in a camper (and what wasn't) for our style of camping so we wanted to create one to our own design. We decided on a Vauxhall Vivaro base vehicle as this seemed a good compromise between size and comfort and, in 2016, we bought 'Big Red'. He was a crew van in his former life so we had to take the seats out of the back although we have designed the interior so that we can keep one of the belted seats in the back which enables the van to carry four people although two would need to sleep in a tent (or buy one of those clever roof-top bedrooms). We also use this belted seat with the table to work on our laptops while we are away. I sometimes take the van away by myself to write and sitting by the window at my 'workstation' with a great view is really inspiring.

Before we designed Big Red, we really had to think about how we were going to use him and what were the most important things to us and what we could compromise on. Just like buying a house, there is always some degree of compromise to buying a campervan and even if you had a deluxe motorhome which has everything, you would be compromising on where you could drive, park and on fuel economy.

So, in my opinion, the first thing you need to think about if you are going to buy or convert your own campervan is - what sort of camper are you?

'Going camping' can mean many different things - from those minimalist campers who travel with everything on their pushbike and camp in the woods in a tent the size of a teabag, to those people who park up in an enormous, deluxe RV fit for a celebrity. Neither are right or wrong, just different strokes for different folks.

Five Styles of Camping

However, if you are choosing the campervan route, I think there are probably five main camping styles:

Day Camping: where you just want a comfortable place to sit/make a cup of tea while you are out for the day. In this case, insulation/ventilation are not really going to be an issue although you will need to think about how you are going to generate power for your cooking. Probably a simple, single gas burner will do the job for making cups of teas alongside a BBQ for cooking meals outside. You won't need a lot of storage and a single leisure battery will probably do for a bit of 12V lighting, a cool box and to charge phones/tablets.

Week Camping: where you want to camp for up to a couple of weeks for, say, a dozen times throughout each spring/summer/autumn and you need a fairly good bed, some inside seating and reasonable cooking facilities. In-van toilet facilities (even if is just for night-time) are also something you might want to consider if your van has space. If you are going to extend your vanning time into the winter, you will also need to think about some serious heating.

Month Camping: where you go on longer trips that take you away from home for a month to six months and in different climates. Now you want a proper bed, a stand-up interior, comfortable in-van cooking, a proper fridge, some loo/bathroom facilities, some serious heat regulation and some decent seating. You'll probably also want a bit more storage. This type of camping is probably mostly done by the retired community or young couples taking some time out.

Year Camping: Where you want to do have a mega adventure and go off in the van for a year or two. Now you need everything you have in the Month Camping section plus a lot more storage. In this situation you may also want to work from the van so you may need to think about a comfortable workstation of some kind. This style of campervanning is mainly done by free-spirit 20-somethings or intrepid young families.

Live-in camping: This is where you choose to live in your van as a permanent thing and so is not really camping but is a whole lifestyle in itself. This is not something that I have experienced myself so I can't really comment on the challenges and requirements of this lifestyle. However, there are plenty of vanlifers who put up videos on YouTube with helpful advice on living in a campervan.

Of course, I realise that everyone is different, and some people are happy to go away for months in a week-style camper, but I am just mentioning the ideal here. A couple of my friends went away to Scotland for a couple of months in a tiny Nissan NV200 and had a great time!

Although Glyn and I would like to be *Month Campers*, work constraints mean that we can only be *Week-Campers* at this point in our lives, and we also need our camper to be our second vehicle so we knew this campervan had to be at the smaller end of the spectrum.

Another major consideration that you need to think about, no matter what your camping style is, is how much you are going to be camping at campsites and how much you'll be doing wild camping. This has a big impact on how you are going to power your van as if you are wild camping you won't have EHU (electric hook-up). This will also be true if you are using your van a lot for festivals. Also, if you want to do a lot of stealth camping, you will need to choose a van that doesn't look like a campervan too.

(Stealth camping is the art of camping in wild or urban places, without detection. For some people, it is the covert nature of stealth camping which gives it its appeal and excitement. It often allows you to explore amazing places in an intimate and inexpensive way.)

The Money Thing

And then, of course, there is the question of budget which may be part of the deciding factor in what sort of camper you can be at this stage. If you are buying a ready-made campervan then you clearly just have to decide what price you can pay although you may want to have a little extra cash spare to do any repairs or updates to the van. If you are buying a vehicle to convert, then obviously you have to think about conversion costs and that will depend on whether you are going to do it yourself or give the van to professional converters to do. But more of that in **Chapter 4**.

3. Try before you buy

This is probably the most important piece of advice you will take away from this book - if you have never owned a campervan before, it is a really good idea to hire one for, at least, a weekend before you even consider buying one. Even if you have been a tent-camper for many years it is still a good idea to do this.

As I mentioned previously, I got hooked on the campervanning life when Glyn and I hired a motorhome on a Groupon for a week. It wasn't the best campervanning experience in the world as it was an older model and a bigger vehicle than we really wanted, but it was enough to know that we did want a smaller campervan in our lives.

Although we had been tent-campers for some years, I had never really thought about getting a campervan - it just wasn't on my radar. However, when we had our week away in the motorhome I was completely smitten, and I was quite shocked at how emotional I felt about it all. I was not prepared for the effect it had and it felt like a missing piece of my life jigsaw had been found. I wouldn't have known this if we hadn't tried out the motorhome deal and my life would have taken a very different direction and been far less fulfilling.

Campervans Are Trendy

Of course, it can go the other way too. People who think they really want a campervan can try it and absolutely hate it.

At the time of writing (2019), campervans are becoming very popular and even trendy. On the talent show TV program, The X Factor, there is always an audience competition and the prize is usually a chunk of money and a vehicle. It used to be a luxury car but, at the moment, it is a VW campervan. Like I say, campervans are trendy now.

So, people who might never have considered any type of camping before now want to own a campervan, maybe just because of the trend. It may well be that these people do end up loving the campervan life but I have known of families and couples who spend £40,000 on a super-styled VW camper and then use it 4 times before they want to sell it.

Then there is the fact that sometimes, when it comes to couples, one member can fall in love with campervanning and the other is just not into it at all. In fact, some people can feel absolutely tortured by the idea of a few nights in a campervan. In my experience it is often the wives/girlfriends who are not keen, and I totally respect that not everyone is comfortable with communal showers or peeing in a glorified bucket. However, this is not always the case. There are plenty of women out there who absolutely relish the freedom and contact with nature that you get on a campervan trip and plenty of guys who prefer a comfortable hotel if travelling at all. I often wonder what it is in a person that makes them light up at the thought of a camping adventure and for others it just feels like endurance. I guess it must have something to do with the free-spirit thing.

However, if both partners are not equally keen that is not the end of the world so long as one person is not totally traumatised by the idea of camping. My partner is not as besotted by the campervan experience as I am, but he does enjoy going on camping trips throughout the summer. To get my extra fix, I will sometimes take the van away by myself to do some writing or to meet up with a friend.

So, you do want to make sure that, before you invest a lot of money in a campervan, you and all your co-travellers are equally (or nearly equally) keen on the idea and you can't really know this until you try it.

Voyage of Discovery

Hiring a campervan for a few days can also help you decide what sort of camper you are and get an idea of the sort of van that suits you best. For example, if you are both tall people, you may find that you really need a high roof van and a fixed bed across the width of the van is just simply not long enough.

You'll also get to cook in the van and find out what your eating style is and therefore what sort of kitchen you need or don't need. Do you like cooking inside the van or do you much prefer cooking outside? Do you need 2 rings, a grill and an oven or are you happy with one ring that can be moved inside and outside the van? What sort of fridge do you need: a 3-way condensing fridge or just an electric cool box?

You'll also get to answer other questions like:

- **Do you need an awning and if so what sort of awning do you need (see Chapter 14)**

- **Do you like driving a van and what is important about the drive for you: cruise control, air con, automatic/manual, sensors/reversing camera, fuel economy, easy to park.**

- **What sort of campsites do you prefer and are you keen to do wild camping as well?**

• **What sort of bedding do you need to have to feel warm and comfortable?**

• **What sort of clothes do you need to take and how will you store them?**

This is a valuable opportunity to try it all out for real and some of what you discover may well surprise you.

For many people, this may well set you off on a frenzied search for your first van (yay!) and you will suddenly become addicted to YouTube, Pinterest, Autotrader and Gumtree, but in a good way.

For others you may well think that once was enough, and you have saved yourself the angst and expense of buying an expensive possession that you then have to get rid of.

But, whatever you decide in the end, it is a journey of discovery worth taking as you may well find that you have discovered something that brings more joy into your life than you thought possible.

4. To convert or not to convert, that is the question?

So now you come to the time when you need to make the decision of whether you want to buy a campervan that is already converted, or do you want to buy an empty van and convert it yourself?

There are pros and cons to both choices, and these are what I think they are:

Buying a Ready-made Campervan

The Pros:

- You don't have to convert it! This means that you can go camping in it straight away. Yay!
- If you are a couple, you might avoid potential divorce! Of course, everyone is different and for some couples I know the conversion process has been a relationship-enhancing experience. But if you think about what it is like renovating a house, then converting a campervan is similar and you may naturally experience some similar stresses and strains along the way.
- In some cases, it may be cheaper than converting it yourself.
- Ideally, it will already have Campervan status with DVLA so it should be cheaper to insure.

The Cons:

- The van may not be exactly to your taste or best for your style of camping and you may find that you want to sell it on fairly quickly.
- You may not be able to afford the campervan you *really* want
- No matter how much you love your van, you will never feel about it the way that you will feel about it if you have converted it yourself.
- You will miss the opportunity to learn some new skills

If you have decided on the readymade route than you will need to first decide on your budget. Also, will you buy it outright or are you going to go the finance route, in which case, what sort of monthly payments can you afford? Then I suggest going through this book and asking yourself the questions in here before you start even looking at vans. If there is more than one person who is going to use/choose the van, you may want to go through the questions together as you don't want to make an 'arse-umption' about what the other person is thinking and then find out later that they want something completely different to you! And, in my experience, just as with house hunting, when you are van hunting if both buyers are not on the same page then the right house/van will never appear and if it does, something will happen to sabotage the sale.

You may then want to go to some of the motorhome/campervan shows and just have a look at the vans there as you can go inside them and get a feel for how that design might work for you. Would a standard rock & roll bed be big enough/comfortable enough for you? Are you OK with the headroom in that particular van or would standing height be important to you? Stand at the cooker and imagine yourself cooking - does that design work for you? How would it be if it was lousy weather and you were stuck inside that van for a while? When you are in each van, try and imagine how you will, sleep, sit, cook, store in it in all weathers. You might be surprised how this changes your mind about what you THOUGHT you wanted.

Try not to be too sucked-in by all the glossiness - one professional converter once confided in me that a lot of conversions are done to look fantastic in the showroom but are not that practical once you get out camping.

You could also visit some van dealers to just get a feel for the van vehicle itself on their forecourts. Make sure that all the drivers can easily drive the type of van that you might choose. I am only 5ft tall and I do struggle a bit with changing gears in our Vivaro, not that it isn't a nice van to drive, it is great (especially as it is a 2.5 litre!) but only having little arms and legs makes it a bit of a stretch. However, Glyn fits just fine and loves driving it! We are already planning our next van now and have decided that the new one will be something that drives more like a car.

It is also a good idea to go online and look at second-hand campervans for sale on places like Gumtree and Facebook groups to get an idea of the prices of vans that do not come out of showrooms or dealers. If you are buying a van in this way, unless you are a bit of a mechanic yourself, it would be good to take someone with experience with you when you find a van you are serious about to check out the van for mechanical/bodywork soundness. Of course, ask to see the service history and check the latest MOT certificate for advisories.

Converting an Empty Panel Van/Vehicle

The Pros:

- You will have a van that is exactly right for you and your style of camping.
- You will have a special bond with this van that is inexplicably heart-warming
- You may be able to create the campervan that you couldn't afford
- You will learn skills that will be useful in other parts of your life
- You will be part of a converters community and get to meet some lovely, supportive people.

The Cons:

- You will have to spend a lot of weekends doing DIY often in the cold (unless you are lucky enough to be one of those people that has a large workshop but for most self-build converters that is not the case).
- You won't be able to use it straight away although most of us self-converters use our campervans long before they are complete.
- Sometimes things WILL go wrong, and it can be frustrating and tiring.
- When it comes to older campervans, you may spend more money converting than you would if you bought one that was already converted although a lot depends on the fittings you choose and how skilled you are at DIY already.
- You will need to apply for Campervan (Motor Caravan) status with DVLA yourself.

If you have decided to convert an empty van then the first question you need to ask yourself is will you hand it over to professional converters or will you convert it yourself?

Using Professional Converters

There are now a growing number of professional campervan converters around the country who have large workshops often in slightly rural places. They are not always so easy to find but most of them have a Facebook page and you can see their previous work and get a feel of their vibe. But it is always best to visit them and have a chat before even considering them for your van. Most of them are nice, soulful guys but, because there is more work than converters, you can sometimes feel like you are engaging an artiste rather than a contractor.

Then, if it feels right and you have the budget, you can simply hand over your vehicle to them and come back a few weeks later to a more or less complete campervan. However, there are a few challenges in this route:

- Professional converters often have a long waiting list - sometimes up to six months!
- Most professional converters like to do standard interiors in which they can just install ready-made kitchen units and beds. Anything bespoke will cost a lot more and take more time if you can get them to take the project on at all.
- The converter will need to have the van at their workshops for probably a few weeks while they convert it.
- It is best to check their previous work and designs to make sure that it is what you want and hopefully talk to one of their previous customers for a recommendation.
- You will need to be prepared to pay somewhere between £7,000 and £15,000 for a general conversion.

Converting the Van Yourself?

There is no way to really prepare you for self-converting a campervan. It is one of those things, probably a bit like having a baby, that, no matter how much somebody describes it to you, until you have experienced it you cannot really know. Actually, the baby analogy is quite a good one as you are giving birth to something. The sort of questions you need to ask yourself before diving into this experience are:

- Are you prepared for the agony and the ecstasy? Self-build converting, like any creative process, has its highs and lows
- How much time have you got to spend on working on the van around your work/family life?
- Where are you going to work on the van (workshop, garage, drive, road or, in our case, sometimes on the kitchen floor!)?
- What sort of DIY skills do you have (or not have) and do you actually enjoy DIY?
- How many tools do you already have (power drill, saw, jig saw, workbench, sander, plus lots of other bits and pieces) and how many will you have to buy? Do you know how to use them?
- Do you have skilled family and friends with tools who can help?
- Do you need to have the van ready by a certain date and can you get the van to a liveable state by then?
- How much do you have to spend on the conversion? Have you done some initial research to get an idea of how much van interiors cost? (For example, a new rock & roll bed can cost you anything from £500 to £2,000). Of course, if you have the skills (and if you were like us, even if you didn't have the

skills) you can create your own pull out bed from timber.

- Who is going to design the layout and source the materials? In an ideal situation you would have one person who is mainly the designer and one who is mainly the DIY master and you share ideas together. If you are both designers or both DIY bods, then you may have to think about how the team is going to work. If you are converting alone then you have to be both.
- Do you want to do a hybrid conversion? By this I mean do you want to project manage the build yourself but use skilled craftsmen for some of the jobs like: electrics, carpentry and upholstery. However, a word of caution here. Converting a van requires extra skills to building work in a house. We started our conversion with a skilled builder/craftsman who gave up halfway through because, even though he was very good at most of the building skills, he couldn't see how to join and connect things in the campervan.

Self-converting a Campervan: A General Job list

1. Design the Van

So, you have an empty panel van - but where do you start? You will need to create some sort of preliminary design for your van which, I can assure you, will change as you go along but you do need to have some kind of blueprint to start with. There are design apps and packages that you can use to do a virtual layout of a space and if you are tech inclined it might be helpful to use one of these. Otherwise you could create a scaled-down floor plan on a piece of paper and then build to scale 3D bits of furniture out of cardboard to put on the floorplan, a bit like a dolls house!

You can then move the micro furniture around to see the best configuration or if you can actually fit the bed/kitchen/shower in at all. Some people build life-sized bits of furniture from cardboard and create an actual layout around them so that they can physically stand and move around their 'campervan'.

2. **Clear the Van**

Sometimes this isn't necessary because the van is empty but often there will be panels and/or a bulkhead to remove as a minimum. Our Vivaro was a crew van so it had some metal racking in the back which had to be unscrewed from beneath the vehicle which was a bit of a pain. If you are buying a vehicle that was previously a disabled vehicle you may need to take out lifting equipment and special seating. If you are converting something like an ex-ambulance/police vehicle there will be specialist equipment to remove and you need to check how it is attached to the vehicle.

3. **Insulate the Van**

I don't know why, but I just love insulating a van! There is something very satisfying about putting fluffy, warm stuff on the walls, ceiling and floor and I was amazed at the difference in touch temperature between the bare metal and the insulated surfaces in our van. I am a big fan of Dacron. Dacron is the white, woolly-looking material that most converters use as the inner lining of their van. It is a polyester fibre which, unlike natural fibres, is non-absorbent, and is mildew-resistant (really important in a van). One night when we were camping in the van before it was finished it was pretty cold and I wrapped some spare Dacron around my feet, and I was as warm as toast! In our van we have also found another use for the Dacron in the bed. We have stuck a layer of Dacron to one side of the foam base that we are using for the bed so that we can use that side to sleep on if it is a cold night. It also makes the cushion more rounded and look better. However, before you go mad with the Dacron on the van walls it is usual to cover the bare metal with some sort of insulating matting or Celotex board with a silver radiant barrier on one side of it. We used a product that was a bit like a yoga mat with a silver side for our van. As it was self-adhesive it made life a lot easier as I didn't have to use spray glue. (WARNING on spray glue: make sure that you get one that can cope with higher temperatures as you don't want it all melting when the sun is on the van for a few hours). However, there are all sorts of products that you can use to insulate a van so you will need to do a bit of research first.

4. Lining the Van

Oohh, now we come to the pretty bit. Once you have insulated the van you then need to think about what wall finishings you will have. But first you will need to fix a ply board lining over the insulation to which you can attach your covering of choice and furniture. Many people choose to cover their walls in van carpeting which is a stretchy kind of felt material that comes in large rolls. You will need to cut the material to size and then glue it on the walls with a spray glue and roller to make sure that you get a nice flat finish. I would really recommend getting 4-way stretch carpeting as it makes application a lot easier. The other most common finish for campervan walls/ceiling is wood strips although, in my opinion, in a small van this can begin to look a bit like a sauna if you overdo it. For the floor you will need to choose something that stays looking good even when walked on in wet boots. It will also have to cope as a kitchen floor but look nice enough for a bedroom.

5. Installing an Electrical System

Now, I am no expert on this subject and, although I did quite a bit of research on this, I still would not feel confident to do it all myself although I have met people who are not experts but still do a great job but you do have to consider the safety side, of course. The way we did it in Big Red was to buy a complete electric pack from a reputable supplier and our builder fitted it to first-fix stage and we finished it off by adding the light fittings.

In a campervan your electrical supply usually includes both mains hook-up and 12v electrics running off the leisure batteries, so you do really need to think about what is going to run off what before you start buying the kit (see **Chapter 15**). It is also best to decide on whether you will have solar panels to charge the leisure batteries at this stage too so you can fit all the wiring and controllers before you finish the walls. Rayne Automotive, who supplied our electric pack were incredibly helpful and cut it all to my design, so it arrived ready for installation with a schematic drawing. They were also helpful further down the line when we needed to extend some of the wiring. So, you need to decide whether it is worth it to you to learn all the electrics yourself or maybe buy a pre-designed basic pack and then fit that.

6. Fitting Furniture

In a campervan, the furniture that you need is mainly for sleeping, sitting, eating, bathroom and cooking. You can buy all of these items as ready-made furniture units, like rock & roll beds, sink/cooker units, portapotti, shower units and tables that fit into the floor or walls. However, these can be expensive, and you will need to make sure that they will all fit in to the space you have in the van.

Otherwise you can make your own or adapt existing furniture (I know one guy who fitted out most of his van with modified IKEA furniture).

7. **Fitting Windows.**

For a van to get Campervan status with the DVLA, it needs to have at least one window in the load area. Usually the windows are already tinted but, if not, you will need to get this done. You will also need to fit curtains at the windows.

8. **Installing Heating**

This depends a lot on individual preference and whether you want to use your van in the depth of winter or in colder climates. If you are on hook-up using mains electricity, then you can plug in any type of portable electric heater that you might use at home. If you want to be able to heat the van when you are wild camping, then you will need to have something that uses gas or diesel but more of that later.

So, as you can see, converting your own campervan does require a lot of different DIY skills. For some people who are already skilled or know somebody with skills who can help it does make it a lot easier, but I am always amazed at what non-DIY people have achieved in their self-build campervans.

5. Choosing the Base Vehicle

Aahhh, now we come to choosing the actual VAN. This is more important than many people think as it is very easy to get carried away with the glossy interiors, or planning your interior design if you are converting, and the actual vehicle tends to slide in to the background a bit. But, I think, it is a bit like buying a house in that the van is similar to the location of the property and the fitout is like the interior decor of the house. You can always change the space inside a house by extending or renovating, but you can't change the location unless you up and move. The same with a campervan, you can always change the interior, but the van is the van. So, here are the things that I think are important to consider when choosing your campervan vehicle:

- Size of vehicle
- What model of van works best for you?
- What age of van can you afford and what mileage will you accept?
- Is it mechanically/structurally sound?
- Who is going to drive it?
- Does this need to be a second vehicle?
- Overseas Travel
- Where are you going to park it?
- Number of Passengers
- Do You Intend to do Stealth Camping in it?

- Are You Going to Have an Awning?

Before we start answering these questions it's good to remember that there is no right or wrong in your choices - only what is right or wrong for YOU. One of the joys of the campervan world is that there are so many different types of campervan - from an estate car with a roof bedroom (I actually met a lovely, Scandinavian couple who had camped this way with their 3 children for many years!) through to a super-deluxe apartment-on-wheels with an extending bedroom or an elevating bed! All are equally OK.

Size of Vehicle

At first glance you might think that bigger is better, but this is not always the case when it comes to campervans. It is always a balance between living space and ease of driving/parking.

There are six, main 'types' of vehicle that are used as motorhomes/campervans:

1. Micro-camper Conversions (Car-derived Campers)

I have a real soft spot in my heart for micro-campers. Our first camper was a micro camper - a Toyota Previa called 'Trev-the-Prev' and we had some great adventures in him. Most micro campers are created from a people-carrier style car or a mini-van and I have seen some really clever conversions that make great use of the limited space. The sort of vehicles that make good micro campers are: Renault Kangoo, Fiat Doblo, Citroen Berlingo, Peugeot Partner, Skoda Yeti, VW Caddy or Caravelle, Mercedes V-class, Toyota Proace and, of course, for those on a smaller budget, older vehicles like our Toyota Previa. For many of these micro vans, you can buy an instant conversion kit that you can load in to the back which gives you the basics like bed, seating, table and these can be lifted in and out so you can still use your vehicle in its normal mode for most of the time and just convert it for your trips. Check out the *Amdro Boot Jump.*

The advantages of a micro camper are that they are very easy to drive on all roads and can park in all the usual places. They are often economical to run, are often less expensive to buy than their larger siblings but that is such a variable and depends a lot of age, mileage, brand etc.

The obvious disadvantage is the lack of space and height. This is not a problem when the weather is fine but presents a challenge when you have wet/cold weather and need to be inside. However, in my opinion, having a good awning can solve a lot of that problem and it would certainly not put me off having a micro camper.

2. **Panel Van Conversions**

These are any of the typical 'workmen' vans that are designed for commercial use but are converted into a campervan by insulating, lining, adding electrical power systems and fitting out with scaled-down furniture. They can vary a lot in size and, I think, there are two categories of panel vans: small/medium and long. Again, it's all a compromise between living space and drive/parkability (and fuel costs of course). The long panel vans do give you plenty of house space, especially useful if the van is sleeping more than two people, and there is also the potential for a proper bathroom but they are less manoeuvrable and will not park in a normal parking space which can be challenging at times. You decide.

Typical panel vans include: VW Transporters, Vauxhall Vivaro, Renault Trafic, Nissan Primastar/NV200, Ford Transit/Connect/Custom, Mercedes Sprinter/Vito,

Renault Master, the Iveco range, Peugeot Boxer/Expert, Citroen Relay/Despatch, Fiat Ducato.

Most of the smaller panel vans have limited head height so converters will often put a pop-top in the roof which means the roof can go up when you are parked and come down when you are travelling allowing you can get in to most car parks. The other advantage of most panel vans is that they can go pretty much anywhere that a general car can go and this is especially useful when you are out on small country lanes that lead to fantastic beaches!

The other advantage of panel vans is that, unless you pimp-up the exterior, they still look like an everyday commercial van which makes stealth camping and wild camping easier. (Remember, stealth camping is the act of secretly camping in a public or private area and moving on the next morning without being detected.)

3. **Coachbuilt Motorhomes**

These are what you traditionally think of as the typical white Motorhome. They are purpose-built for camping and are like an adapted caravan unit that has been put on a lorry chassis with a cab, a bit like a snail's shell. Some of them have a loft space over the cab where you can sleep but, the only time I slept in an over-cab bed I felt like I was sleeping in an MRI scanner so it was not for me. However, these vehicles do offer a level of space and comfort that you don't normally get in a converted panel van although their size can restrict your adventures when it comes to exploring out- of-the-way places.

4. **A-Class**

These are like a full caravan unit which has been added on top of an engine/chassis, so it gives maximum space. The square shaped, Hymer range are typical of this type of motorhome. These vehicles are deluxe in design and interiors and tend to be quite pricey and, again, you do sacrifice accessibility to out-of-the-way places and easy parking spaces. Many are also over 3.5 tonnes in weight so you will need to check your licence entitlements before committing to buy one of these. If you passed your test after 1st January 1997 you might need to take extra tests to drive vehicles weighing between 3.5 tonnes and 7.5 tonnes. To drive a motorhome with a MAM (Maximum Authorised Mass = vehicle + contents) in this weight range you will need to have a category C1 licence. You can go to www.gov.uk/guidance/driving-a-van to check your licence entitlements.

5. **RV (Recreational Vehicles)**

These are mostly BIG and found in the USA where they have wider, straighter roads that go for miles and miles so having a huge vehicle isn't a problem. RVs are pretty much like an apartment on wheels and are bigger and pricier that most UK motorhomes but, in my opinion, while giving you a very deluxe living experience, are not really practical for camping around Europe.

6. **Anything goes**

In theory, any vehicle could be converted into a camping home. A friend of mine used to convert her Ford Fiesta into a nano camper when she was away in it by simply flattening the front seat and putting a piece of thick foam down the length of the vehicle to make a single bed. She has also made some cute 'blinds' that can be stuck to the windows and has a small gas camping stove to cook on. She didn't do a lot of camping then, but this worked for her to give her somewhere to sleep when she went away on her art courses. However, I do have to tell you that she has now bought a ready-converted van... and so the addiction begins!

So, anything is possible. The unusual vehicles that are also sometimes converted into campervans are: ambulances, police vehicles, horseboxes, ex-army vehicles, jeeps, or buses.

For the purposes of this book, I will focus mainly on micro-campers and panel van conversions but many of the principles and questions that you would need to ask yourself before choosing a camping vehicle will apply to motorhomes too.

What Model of Van Works Best for You?

Once you start researching vans you will realise that there are many different variations on the basic model of a van. There are different lengths and heights, and these are written as L1H1 (Length 1, Height 1) which is the smallest version of the van. You can then get L1H2 (short length, higher height) or L2, H2 which is the longer and high-top version of the van. One of the critical decisions when you are choosing a campervan is the height: is it important to be able to stand up fully in it or are you ok with a vehicle that is not full head height? Of course, many converted vans have a pop-top already installed which allows you to stand up when you are parked, although remember that most pop-tops are fabric so can make the van colder and can be a problem in high winds although most people take the roof down at night for sleeping. If you are buying a van to convert yourself then putting a pop-top in it would cost around £2,000.

An H2 hard-top vehicle can give you great headroom and extra storage space but may not be able to get under some of the height restriction barriers in supermarket/public car parks. Again, it is a compromise and you need to decide what is most important to you.

Some manufacturers talk about SWB (short wheelbase) and LWB (long wheelbase) versions of their van. Our Vivaro is the SWB version, the LWB has a load area that is 40cm longer but is the same height as the SWB.

Each manufacturer has their own version of a SWB or L1,H1 (Length 1, Height 1) design so you really need to look up the load area dimensions of any van that you are interested in. As with our Vivaro, 40cm extra length doesn't sound like much but in a campervan it can make a big difference, especially when you remember that this is 3D so is a whole extra block of space. It can be the difference between having some floor space at night when the bed is down or not having any floor space when the bed is down. In fact, if we decide to convert a Vivaro again we have decided that we would get the LWB version as it makes a significant difference to the living space without changing much in the driving/parking function. Honestly, there are so many different variations within each van model that you really have dive deep on the model of your choice to see what variations there are and what works best for you.

Anyway, here is a general sample of some van load area dimensions to give you an idea of what to look for:

Short Wheelbase, Low Roof (L1, H1) - Length 2.5m, height 1.4m, width 1.7m

Long Wheelbase, Low Roof (L2, H1) - Length 2.9m, height 1.4m, width 1.7m

Long Wheelbase, High Roof (L2, H2) - Length 2.9m, height 1.9m, width 1.7m

Medium Wheelbase - Length 3.4m, height 1.9m, width 1.8m

Long Wheelbase - Length 4.3m, height 1.9m, width 1.8m

Long Wheelbase Maxi - Length 4.8m, height 1.9m, width 1.8m

What Age of Van can You Afford and What Mileage Will You Accept?

Obviously, the age and mileage of a van will be reflected in its price so the age-range and mileage level that you will need to accept will depend a lot on the budget you have.

The Age Thing

From the perspective of reliability, running costs and maintenance, a younger van is better. The classic VWs do look very cute but you do almost need to be a mechanic to drive one as they are prone to engine problems unless the vehicle has had a new engine put in it. You also do have to adopt a more laidback style of driving in these vans as they won't race up the motorway, which, of course, is fine for some people. In the excellent BBC 2, TV program, 'One Man and His Campervan', Martin Dorey filmed his travels around the country in a classic VW and he did need to be towed home at the end of the series so do be aware that with the classic van comes the mechanical challenges.

If you are going for an older converted panel van, then maintenance can have its challenges too. Not only are you likely to need to do more of it, it can sometimes be more difficult to find the parts. I have known van owners who have experienced this with their older vans so do check out the parts situation before committing to an older van - it doesn't need to be a deal-breaker but just be aware of what you are taking on.

Certain makes of vans are prone to different types of maintenance challenges. I'm afraid that I have been told by several mechanics and van dealers that Ford vehicles are prone to rust in the bodywork, and older vans generally may present bodywork issues. One of the reasons we went for the Vivaro is that they have a galvanised body so do not rust.

When it comes to running costs, you will generally be paying more for an older van. Most vans run on diesel and, at the time of writing, European governments are looking to penalise diesel vehicles in the future even though, in the past, they were praised for their fuel economy (go figure!). Because of the exhaust emissions, you will also pay more in road tax (Vehicle Excise Duty) for an older van so before buying a van do check its Euro number. Both cars and vans have a Euro rating which ranges from Euro 1 to Euro 6 (at the moment) and this relates to the how clean or how dirty the emissions are. Since 1992, European Union regulations have been imposed on new vehicles, with the aim of improving air quality - meaning a vehicle has to meet a certain Euro emissions standard when it is made. Knowing your vehicle's rating is more important than ever now, as more and more levies and fines are being introduced for older vehicles, especially diesels. The current (2019) Euro rating is Euro 6 which was introduced back in September 2014 so any vehicle registered after that to date should be rated as Euro 6 but they do vary near the changeover date. The higher the Euro number, the better the emissions and the less tax you will pay. However, this is a developing thing and I believe new Euro levels will be introduced in the future. To check out your vehicle's Euro rating go to: eurostandards.co.uk

Beware Low Emissions Zones

On 8th April 2019, the British government introduced a ULEZ (Ultra Low Emissions Zone) which covers the same area as the congestion charge zone in central London. It operates 24 hours a day, 7 days a week, every day of the year and, if your vehicle does not meet their emissions requirements and you enter the zone you will be charged £12.50 a day for vans up to 3.5 tonnes and (unbelievably!) £100 per day for anything over that. For a diesel van to meet their emissions requirements it must be Euro 6 but do check your particular vehicle on the Transport for London website which you can find at

https://tfl.gov.uk/modes/driving/ultra-low-emission-zone/ways-to-meet-the-standard.

There is also a LEZ (Low Emissions Zone) which covers most of Greater London (inside the North and South Circular roads) but mainly affects larger vans, minibuses, lorries, buses and coaches but if you have a long wheelbase vehicle this might be you. It also depends on the date that your van was registered and if your vehicle is categorised as a panel van or a motorised caravan so it is best to check it by registration number on their site. They will be further tightening up on the emissions allowed in this zone in October 2020.

At the moment, Low Emission Zones are only in London, York, Glasgow and Leeds but they are also proposed for Bristol, Bath, Oxford (electric vehicles only), Birmingham, Sheffield, Warrington, Manchester, Newcastle, Edinburgh, Dundee and Aberdeen. If you live within these zones, you are going to be heavily penalised if you want to park an older vehicle there (this applies to petrol cars as well as vans). Please do keep an eye on these emerging new rules on the Transport for London website as above and on

https://www.buyacar.co.uk/cars/economical-cars/523/clean-air-zone-charges-where-are-britains-low-emission-zones

Older Vans are Less Efficient

Also, older vans usually do less miles to the gallon than newer vans, especially compared to the new vans which have an eco-function. This can make a big difference in the cost of your holidays if you are travelling large distances.

However, if your budget only extends to an older van at the moment then don't let it stop you - it is better to have an older campervan than no campervan at all!

Mileage

In theory, the less mileage on a vehicle the better although, if it is brand new, that will mean that you will need to drive it carefully for the first few hundred miles while it is being run-in. However, we bought our Vivaro from a van dealer who is also an ex-mechanic with decades of experience and he said that it is not only the number of miles on the clock that reflect engine wear and tear, it is also the way the van has been driven. A van that has been driven a lot in urban areas (lots of stopping and starting and gear changing) will have an engine that is far more worn that one that has done the same miles on mainly motorways or A roads. He said that the Post Office vans, which are doing constant stopping and starting are pretty worn out by 60,000 miles whereas you can have a van with 200,000 miles on the clock that has been used to smoother use (and good maintenance) that will have an engine that could go for another 100,000 miles! When I first started looking at vans to buy for our camper, it took me quite a while to get used to the fact that vans normally have much higher mileage on the clock than cars do. A car is considered high mileage at 100,000 but with a van, it is just getting going. I've heard of campervans with 500,000 miles on the clock and still going strong but that is unusual.

Bear in mind that, a campervan generally does less miles per year than a normal family/commuting vehicle so having around 100,000 on the clock when you buy a van is no big deal. How long would it take you to put another

100,000 miles on the clock? If you did 5,000 miles a year then that would be 20 years!

In conclusion, it is generally better to buy a younger van with less mileage on the clock but, for many of us, our budget means that we may have to go for a more travelled van. Our first van was a converted 1997 Toyota Previa with 130,000 miles on the clock which we bought for £1,000. We had a great time in 'Trev the-Prev' and he was extremely reliable (they say "You can't kill a Toyota"!) and it was the only way that we could start on the campervan ladder so just buy the best vehicle that you can afford and start your campervan life.

Is it Mechanically/Structurally Sound?

In my opinion, you really, really don't want a disaster van. If you get a van that has a lot of mechanical or structural issues you will spend a lot of time and money getting it sorted out and you will live with the stress of knowing that your van can breakdown at any time. You want a vehicle that you feel you can rely on. Sometimes you will see older vans for sale at what seems a very cheap price but when you look at the issues it has (if the seller is being honest) then you know that this van is going to be more trouble than it's worth. You'll also probably spend more money on repairing it than you would have buying a better, more expensive van in the first place.

Of course, if your budget is limited you will need to buy an older vehicle and sometimes these can naturally have a few minor issues. A van with a scraped front wheel arch or a dent at the back wouldn't put me off as we know that we can find someone to repair that and it won't affect the reliability of the van. However, if it was crumbling with rust I personally would not go there.

And if there are some general maintenance issues that will need to be addressed to get it through the next MOT, like new windscreen wipers or brake pads, then it may be worth taking that vehicle on anyway if you get a generally good feeling about it. However, unless you are a mechanic yourself or have a relative who is, a vehicle with something like a shot gearbox is going to need major, expensive surgery.

I have found that, over time, I have developed an instinct for a good or bad van but I am no mechanical expert and, if I was buying a used van from a private seller, I would still take a mechanical expert along to check it out. If you are buying your van from a reputable dealer then it is likely to be sound (it's not worth their reputation to sell bad vehicles) and you should be given a warranty of a decent length anyway.

You can also get a good idea about the previous life of your prospective van by checking its MOT history on www.gov.uk/check-mot-history before you buy it (you will need the registration number). This is very revealing and you can see what sort of work has been done on the vehicle to get it through its MOTs and therefore how well it has been generally maintained. Also, ideally, you would want to see a service history book for your prospective vehicle, but I appreciate that for older vehicles, a full, service history may not be possible.

Who is Going to Drive it?

You may ask, "Why does this matter?" but, I have found that this can be a factor if one of the drivers is particularly short or tall. Both my partner and I drive the vehicle although he does more of the driving when we are away (he loves driving our Vivaro - it is a 2.5 litre and goes like poo off a stick which makes it a fun drive). We tend to share the driving on the longer journey there and back which means it is less tiring for the drivers. However, as I am only 5ft tall, I do struggle a bit with the controls. I literally have to plunge sideways down to the floor to put the handbrake on and off and anyone watching would probably think I had disappeared! I also struggle a bit to get the clutch fully down and have to sit very close to the steering wheel to do this which means I have a less than comfortable angle on my foot on the accelerator. Also, first gear is a bit of an arm-stretch and none of this is particularly good for my back. I have found ways to overcome it, like wearing shoes with a thick sole, but it is not ideal. I once spoke to a van dealer about this and he said that there are quite a few commercial vans that are a challenge to drive for people under 5ft 4ins so it is always good to test drive your vehicle thoroughly before buying. I had sat in a Vivaro before and felt comfortable but hadn't driven one and it is a whole different thing. My partner is 5ft 8ins and finds the Vivaro very comfortable to drive.

Of course, driving comfort also depends on the age of the van and the newer vans drive more like a car from the controls perspective with a lot tighter gearstick and more compact cockpit.

Does This Need to be a Second Vehicle?

For many couples/families, their campervan has to be their second vehicle which means that, if one partner takes their car to work, then the van is the vehicle that does any other journeys which may also include commuting. In this case you are not going to want to drive a larger van around both from cost and convenience perspectives so you may want to compromise on a smaller campervan.

Overseas Travel

If you are going to be taking your van abroad a lot, the ferry fees are usually more expensive if you have a longer and higher vehicle. This varies with each carrier so you will need to check each before you book although many ferry companies seem to charge more for vehicles over 6m in length. They also count any tow bars or other external extras in the length/height dimensions of the vehicle.

You will also need to know your van's emissions standard (Euro rating) if you travel in other European countries as different cities around Europe are beginning to impose charges for higher emitting vehicles. The RAC says - "Vehicles are identified when they enter specific cities by a colour-coded sticker which is based on your car's Euro emissions standard. The system is currently active in some cities in France, and if you are caught entering a city without one of the stickers - or drive a vehicle which is banned on a particular day - you could face a fine. If you drive a pre-1992 car that doesn't meet any Euro emissions standard (double check with your manufacturer if you're not sure), your vehicle will not be permitted to enter those zones during times when restrictions are in place."

Where are You Going to Park it?

Another essential factor in choosing the size and type of your campervan is where you are going to park it every day. If you have to park it on the road or if it has to fit on your drive, then this will be key in what vans you can consider. If you have a smaller van it is perfectly OK to park it on the street and this is something we do ourselves as we don't have a drive and it is our second vehicle for everyday use. I often visit Bristol and the streets are lined with VW campervans there. If you lived in Bristol, why wouldn't you have a campervan as it's on the edge of the

West country and Wales which are both prime campervan holiday destinations. It's almost rude not to!

Some people rent storage space for their vans throughout the year but you will need to consider how near it is to your home (this is especially important when you are loading it up for a trip) and the security of the site. I know of one couple who rent a small area of a local farm to store their van but it has been broken in to several times, which is soul destroying when it is your precious home-on-wheels.

However, there are dedicated motorhome storage sites/compounds around most countries, and you will need to Google the ones in your area. Many offer a choice of all year round, seasonal or weekly rates but, for year round storage you are probably looking at anything from £350 for the year so you will need to factor this in in your running-costs budget. The advantage of these official compounds is that they are very secure and often have CCTV and many have CaSSOA (Caravan Storage Site Owners Association) accreditations, which can reduce your insurance costs.

Number of Passengers

The size of the vehicle you choose will also depend on the number of people who will, not only sleep in the vehicle, but who will also travel in the vehicle. In Europe, the law says that every passenger must have a seat with a regulation seat-belt which is why you'll see many rock & roll beds which have seat belts attached to them so extra passengers can ride in the back. The rear seats do not have to face forward, but they must have a belt (for your own safety as much as anything). Our Vivaro was a crew van in its former life which means it had some belted seats in the back behind the driver. We removed these seats but kept one which we have turned around to face the back and we use this to sit on when one of us is working at the table on a laptop (or dining). This also means that when we sell the van on (yes, already planning the next one!), the van could travel a family of four as there is a double passenger seat at the front so the van has four belted seats.

Do You Intend to Do Stealth Camping?

If you want to do stealth camping (parking overnight without being detected) then you are going to need to choose a van that looks just like a commercial van so it cannot have any decals (pictures/stripes) on the outside or anything sticking out of the van that shows it might be slept in such as caravan vents, wood burner flues, obvious solar panels.

Are You Going to Have an Awning?

If you are going to have an awning then you may be able to choose a smaller van as the awning will give you an outside room and space to store larger items when you drive off for the day. (**See chapter 14** for more info on awnings)

6. What is your house style?

Interior design, just like most things in life, has trends and fashions. Think of the décor that many houses in the UK had back in the sixties and seventies - loud patterns on wallpapers and carpets and what we would now consider retro furniture (for those Brits out there, I think of the Only Fools and Horses TV series when I think of this style). Compare that to today's contemporary look which tends to be streamline, simpler and cleaner in design with bi-fold doors out on to the garden and open plan living.

Well, campervans have their interior design trends too although there are more variations on a theme as you would expect with so many different vans and types of people being van owners and converters.

When you talk about campervans most people think of the classic VWs, like the T2 Westfalias, which have the standard layout (side kitchen and rock & roll bed) and a generally retro style. This layout has come forward into the newer VW Transporters but in a more glossy, dark-carpet, high-chrome dressing.

Let's Celebrate Personal Choice

One of the deep joys of campervans is that there are many different designs and finishes and it is completely down to personal choice and we should celebrate that. What a hippy-esque, 20-something couple might go for is likely to be very different to what a retired couple in their seventies might like - but who knows!

One of the things I love about the campervan world is that includes people from all walks of life and, as most 'vanners' are free spirits, there are some really clever and quirky designs. To check out some really unusual and creative van interior designs go to www.quirkycampers.com . Quirky Campers, based in Bristol, are a company that is an agent for van owners who want to rent out their campervans and make some money from their vans in the times they are not using it and Quirky only take on the really well done vans that are a bit out of the ordinary. They also have an annual festival (Camp Quirky) in May every year where people who have converted their own vans meet to appreciate and learn from other converters/experts and generally talk van-geek all day. At the festival you can also look around the Quirky Campervans and you get a much better idea of what will work for you once you are actually inside a van.

Unfortunately, at the mainstream Motorhome and Campervan Shows around the country you mainly only get to see the standard, professionally converted designs and it is hard to get a feel for what all the possibilities are.

Of course, if you want to tour all the amazing options for interiors in campervans from your armchair, there is Pinterest and Instagram (I defy you not to get addicted!) and there are many Facebook groups dedicated to all sort of campervans and camping styles.

However, at the time of writing (2019), there seems to be seven main interior design styles for campervans:

1. The Chintzy Cottage

This style tends to be preferred by the ladies, understandably. Inside there are usually a lot of different patterned/floral fabrics for cushions, curtains, coverings, and lots of soft furnishings. The general feel is soft, bright, cosy and comfortable.

2. The Chrome-fest

This style tends to be preferred by the guys, understandably. Often the walls are covered in darker-coloured carpet and the furniture is clean, straight and finished with chrome. There is usually some serious lighting, usually spotlights. Furniture often comes covered in leathers. The general feel is clean, crisp, dark and a little seductive.

3. The 'Sauna'

These vans are lined, walls and ceiling, with wood strips which give it the sauna feel. It does give it that nice Scandinavian cabin vibe, but in my opinion, you do have to be a bit careful with this décor in a small van as it can make it feel very closed in. The general feel is warm, homely, natural and hygge (Danish for cosy).

4. The Whiteout

Very popular at the time of writing (2019) in both the campervan and property worlds. In this style, white is very much the dominant colour and usually the wall, ceiling and furniture are painted white with a few accents of colour. Flooring is usually a light wood laminate and worktops are often left as natural wood. This design does help a smaller space to look bigger. The general feel is clean, bright, minimal and contemporary.

5. The Ranch

In this design there is a lot of natural, varnished timber in the van including lining, ceiling and furniture which makes you feel as though you are in a ranch house. The furniture has a very artisan, bespoke style with unusual handles and knobs, sometimes in dark metal. The general feel is natural, handmade, low-light and rustic.

6. The Hippy Hideout

The first thing you notice about this design is that it is very colourful. Often lots of high-colour and patterned fabrics such as tie-dye and batik. There is no particular design template that is carried throughout the interior - anything goes, and it feels very relaxed. The general feel is eclectic, laidback, arty and mellow.

7. The Stately Home

This van interior says craftsmanship and probably, significant budget. All the furniture has been beautifully finished and made by a craftsman, usually in wood but now we are talking immaculate oak or ash. Cupboard handles and hinges are all very hidden and clever. Walls, ceilings and floors are seamless and fixtures like sinks and cookers are the highest spec and wouldn't look amiss in John Lewis. The general feel is classy, smooth, comfortable and top-end.

Let the Van Decide

Of course, every van is unique and there are many more individual styles and variations on a theme. The strange thing about our Vivaro campervan was that, when we started converting it, I had a very clear idea that I wanted the van to go along the 'Whiteout' road as I really like this style and I thought it would help the van feel a little bigger and brighter. However, as the build went on, the van seemed to take over and the interior is not what I originally planned although, given that it is a red, SWB van I think that what we have ended up with is better. I don't think our van falls exactly in to any of the main categories as I have kept the background colours to grey, white and cream with red accents in the soft furnishings and some fittings and some graphics on window frames and cupboard doors. I guess it is just a quirky camper!

7. Zoning the interior of the van

When we were designing our campervan, we found it really useful to think about the interior of the van as having different 'zones'. This is also helpful if you are looking for a ready-made van as it makes you think in detail about how you are going to use it as a camper and if it will suit your particular style of camping.

In a way, the zones of the van are like the rooms of a house and each has its own particular job to do - a bedroom is for sleeping in, a kitchen for cooking in and a lounge for relaxing/watching TV. In a campervan these zones tend to merge or even double-up (sometimes triple-up) as one multi-tasking zone and may have to be, say, both a lounge and a bedroom and possibly your dining area as well. In my opinion, the really successful vans (and the most practical for actual camping) are those that have been designed to maximise the use of every bit of space in the interior while keeping a feeling of reasonable spaciousness within the van. Not so easy but there are lots of gorgeous ideas on Pinterest that show ways that vanners have found interesting solutions to space use.

One example that I like because it is so simple and easy to create is a way of storing shoes at the door. When you are camping you often don't want to walk your outside shoes through the van yet you do want them readily available and easy to get to on the way out (this is especially true if you have to go out in the dark). In a house you have a hallway or a shoe cabinet but you won't have that in a van but you do want something that gets them off the floor in a way that doesn't take up valuable storage space. The solution I like is where a couple of lengths of bungee-type elastic is stretched across the outside of the kitchen unit and divided in to shoe-width sections. You can slide the shoes in vertically and they are held there which means they are easy to get at when you are coming in and out. Simple but so clever.

Do a Lot of Research

The campervan world has created all sorts of furniture and fittings that make the best use of a small space and, if you are designing your own van, it is a good idea to do a lot of research on this before planning your layout to get the best from the space. You may also want to check out the marine world and Tiny House movement for equipment and furniture as they have also created some great solutions for small spaces. One of the best ways to plan or identify a good layout is to look at the different 'zones' in the van and what will be the primary piece of furniture that you need in each zone.

When I did a short course in interior design many years ago the main point that I took away from it was that each room in a house has a primary fixture around which the rest of the room is designed. For example, in a bedroom you tend to have: a bed, wardrobes, chest of drawers, bedside tables, and maybe other storage but when you are designing the interior you always place the bed first. In a lounge the primary fixture would be the sofa and, in a kitchen, it would be the cooker. The time I spent as a Feng Shui consultant also taught me that you very much need to consider the entrance to the room as well and how one room flows into another.

So, even though you don't have a lot of space to play with, in a campervan you still need to have these concepts in mind whether you are choosing a ready-made van or designing your own.

The Zones in a Campervan

Your campervan is like a condensed version of a house and will probably have many of the facilities that a home has except it will be in micro form so let's take an overview look at each zone now (we will look at them in detail in later chapters).

The Bedroom Zone

Naturally, the bedroom zone will need to include a bed but, in a campervan, the bed often has to be created before we can sleep in it. Some vans are big enough to have a fixed bed but then that raises the question of what is 'big enough' for your bed?

The Kitchen Zone

The type of kitchen that you will need (or not need) will depend on your style of cooking and how much of it you will want to do when you are away. Also, how long you will be going away for in your campervan does inform what type of food preparation and cooking you will need to do.

The Dining Zone

This zone will usually involve some sort of seating and a table. A lot depends on how many people need to dine at once as a dining zone for two people can be very different to a dining zone for four people.

The Lounge Zone

For many smaller vans there will not really be a dedicated lounge zone so this aspect of your campervan home will depend a lot on how you like to 'lounge' when you are camping. Is your idea of camping lounge-time sitting around talking and having a glass of wine, watching TV or maybe playing board games? Or maybe you like to do a combination of all of them.

The Bathroom Zone

Whether you have a bathroom or not in your campervan depends very much on the size of the van and, with most smaller vans, having an actual bathroom is really not an option so you will need to compromise on your washing/loo needs.

In a campervan it is also important how these zones will interact during day mode and night mode. Some zones may become inaccessible in night mode (like can you get to your fridge when the bed is down?) and you will need to consider this, especially if you are self-building your campervan.

General Storage

In a small van, every inch of space counts and you want to make the most of every little bit when you are designing or considering storage. Storage tends to take part in all of the zones but there are four main types of storage that you will need to consider: Outdoor equipment, Kitchen equipment/food, Clothes, and Bedding.

8. The Bedroom

For me, one of the joys of being away in the campervan is having long, cosy, no-stress sleeps so the bed in our van is really important to us. Also, many of the people I talk to who are converting their own vans say that having a comfortable sleeping area was probably the most important thing on their list, too. If you think about it, a campervan is primarily a bedroom on wheels as that is the most important thing we need when we are camping. Cooking/dining can be done outside or we can buy our meals out and bathroom stuff is often done in shower blocks on a campsite (or with a portable shower if you are wild camping). But, unless it is a really warm night and you have a yearning to sleep out under the stars, we will always need the van to provide us with a warm, safe and comfortable bed.

So when you go and look at a ready-made campervan for sale or when you are choosing a van to convert, first look at the bed (or prospective bed area) and mentally walk yourself through a going-to-bed routine in that van. Is it a bed that you can leave made-up and just climb in to at night, or will you have to pull out a section, fill-in a section or add a section to create the full sleeping area? You will then need to make up the bed sheets unless you are just sleeping in sleeping bags. For some people with mobility issues, arthritis or just general back pain, doing all this can be a bit of a nightmare. For other people it doesn't bother them at all, and they would rather do this to have a bigger bed or more space in the van. So, make sure that the bed is going to give you what you need or offer you a compromise that you can live with.

Fixed Bed or Converting Bed?

There are two main types of bed in a campervan and these are known as: a fixed bed or a converting bed.

A **fixed bed** is a wooden/metal bedframe that has (usually) been built across the back width of the van and has an actual mattress on top of it. Depending on the height of the van, the bed platform is usually built quite high to give extra storage space underneath it. The main advantage of this kind of bed is that it is left made-up during the day so you can just climb into it at night in the same way that you would get in to bed at home.

The **Converting bed** is usually some sort of seating that is adapted at night for sleeping. For campervans with a converting bed, the seating area will be adapted by either: pulling out a rock & roll bed, adding a section to the dining booth, sliding out extra panels or just making up the 'sofa' across the back of the van. However, at one of the large campervan shows we visited a few years ago, I did see a bed that formed part of the ceiling by day and hydraulically descended at night into a bed platform. Yes, I did want one! However, for most vanners this will not be realistic either because of space or budget (but I did so-ooo want it) so usually it is one of the other choices.

So you need to decide what you can live with - do you want something that quickly pulls out or are you happy fitting in a missing section manually and adding the cushions? Will a bed across the back of the van be long enough for all the sleepers? I am only 5ft tall so I could probably sleep in the cupboard but, when I slept across the back of our Vivaro van by myself when it was part- converted, I was only just comfortable enough. Anyone of a grown-up height would probably have struggled. However, saying that, I do know that many people sleep in campervan beds that are shorter than they are and seem completely OK with that which only goes to show that everyone is different and you really do have to think about the van just being right for YOU.

Here is a list of the bedroom factors I think that it would be good for you (and your co-sleepers) to think about before choosing/converting your van:

The Bed Itself

Length of Bed: As I mentioned above, the length of the bed could be a critical factor in which campervan you choose, especially if you are 6ft plus, so check the bed dimensions with the seller before you buy. If you are converting a van and want to get Motor Caravan status with DVLA or for insurance/ferry purposes, then your bed will need to be a minimum of 180cm to qualify. Most rock & roll beds extend to 184 cm so meet the required length.

Width of Bed: You also need to consider the width of the bed. Many rock & roll beds are known as ¾ width beds (width around 110cm) and can be quite narrow for two, especially if you are used to a king-sized bed at home. Full-width rock & roll beds can be from 130cm to 150cm; a normal double bed is 137cm width for comparison. Personally, it would drive me mad having to cram into a narrow bed, but some people don't seem to mind. And what might be OK for you for a few nights might not work for a few weeks so, if you are campers that will be away vanning for weeks/months, that is something to consider.

Hardness of Bed: There is also the hardness of the bed to consider. Again, we are all different and some people relish a hard bed, but I would go insane without my memory foam mattress. Some friends of mine who bought a professionally converted Nissan NV200 van, decided to get a memory foam topper for their rock & roll bed as they found it just too hard - and these are people who have camped around the world in tents! So, if you have found your perfect van but it has a hard bed all is not lost, you can get a topper but you do need to consider where you are going to store it during the day.

Preferably, before you even go looking for a van or if you have found a van you *might* want to buy, I suggest you mark out an area on your lounge floor which is the size of the bed in your prospective van and you both lie down in that space to see what it feels like.

If you are planning to create your own bed from some sort of foam base, do get a sample of the foam and actually *lie on it*. Just pushing it down with your hand really cannot give you an idea of what it would be like to sit/lie on it and it is a very expensive mistake if you get it all covered and then find that it just doesn't work.

The 'Bedology'

Now we come to what sort of bedding you will use and how you will store it (what I call 'The Bedology'). There are a few questions to consider when it comes to creating your Bedology:

To Share or not to Share: If you are a couple, do you want to share the duvet or do you want your own one? Glyn and I have different temperature requirements and, if you are the smaller person, you tend to lose out when it comes to duvet sharing anyway so we have our own duvets .However, this does make the duvets easier to store. If you are going with sleeping bags then you will probably have your own already.

This may sound incredibly decadent, but I have a silk-filled duvet which I just love. It is warm, light and folds down to a small size. It is also a very healthy filling to sleep under. They cost around the same price as a down duvet, which is also a good choice for a campervan. However, if you are going down the duck down route, just make sure that you are not allergic to the filing before you invest in one.

Layers for all weathers: Depending on when and where you are camping, you may need extra warmth for a colder night or something cooler for a very warm night. The fact is, when you are camping, you never really know what temperatures you will get from night to night, so it is best to have a flexible bedding system. I always take a blanket and I love the Teddy Bear blankets that Dunelm sell. They are light, super-warm and wash easily. You can also wrap them around you if you are sitting outside chatting under the stars at night. They even do Teddy Bear fabric onesies, but that may be a step too far. A tip for if the nights turn super-warm: just take your duvet out of its cover and use the cover as a sheet or open your sleeping bag right up and use it as a duvet.

Pillows: Make sure that you have a pillow that really supports your head well at night as a rubbish pillow can lead to back problems in the morning. (It is always a good idea to do a few stretching exercises in the morning when you are camping as you are often doing movements that you don't normally do at home or in the office, especially if you are doing a sport too). I like the memory foam contour pillows, which take a bit of getting used to, but are great for keeping you in the right position in a less than ideal bed.

Bedding Storage: Obviously, all of this bedding needs to be stored during the day when the van is in day mode. Sleeping bags will squash down into their round bags although this is a faff that I just can't be bothered with. If you have a duvet, find an appropriately-sized bag that the duvet can squash in to and you can then use it as a cushion during the day or when you are watching TV or catching up on Netflix in the evening. You can buy duvet storage bags on Amazon for around £7-£10 but make sure that it is made of breathable fabric. We use our pillows as cushions when we're doing a 'boxset binge'.

Places to Put Your Personal Things: You may also want to think about what you need easy access to when you are in bed. Do you need to have a place to put your glass of water, cup of tea or glass of beer if you are 'lounging'? Will you need a little draw/box for things like tissues, ear plugs, medication or other personal stuff?

9. The Kitchen

Now we come to my favourite subject - cooking in a campervan. As The Camper Cookie, I have spent a long time researching recipes and gadgets for cooking tasty and healthy meals when you are camping and it's amazing how many clever gadgets there are out there for camping cooking. But, again, everybody is different, and you may just want to eat out most of the time when you are away in the van. However, if you are going away for weeks at a time this becomes expensive and impractical so you may want a more real kitchen and more extensive cooking kit for your campervan.

In many campervans the kitchen is usually one unit that comprises a 2-ring hob and a sink that is fed by some kind of water container underneath in the unit or built in to the van with its waste water container separate. The kitchen unit is often at the entrance of the van although it can also be at the back of the van so you will open the back doors to cook which is great in good weather but challenging if it is not. However, our first campervan was a micro camper (professionally-converted Toyota Previa) which had a rear kitchen and, because it had a tailgate, I could cook quite comfortably there in a light shower and, if the weather was too bad, we would just go to the pub to eat or have a sandwich. You always find a way.

If you are going to cook inside you will need to be able to stand up in the van whether that is because you have chosen a high top or you have a pop-top. When you consider your cooking zone, you'll also need to think about how you will prepare food and store the equipment that you need so that it is easily accessible.

Kitchen Questions I would ask myself before buying/converting a van...

What is your eating-style when you are away camping? Do you eat out most of the time so only really need to make breakfast and the occasional evening meal? Do you make breakfast and evening meal at the van but eat lunch out? Do you eat most of your meals at the van and take sandwiches for lunch when you are out having adventures?

What is Your Cooking Style? Most people will cook in the same style as they cook at home when they are away camping so it is unrealistic to think that you will suddenly be doing meals that you have not done before, except maybe doing a bit more barbequing. This is why I encourage people to always try my camping recipes at home before they attempt them in the van as it is much easier to experiment first in a familiar kitchen than try it for the first time in your camper kitchen. I personally like to cook mostly one-pan (or maybe two-pan) recipes at home and don't do an awful lot of meals in the oven. Most vans will not have an oven anyway and if your van does have one then you probably have a full kitchen set-up in your van so can cook as if you were at home anyway. When I was having a chat with an Adria motorhome dealer, he told me that often his customers would come back to them a few years later to exchange their van for a newer version and that he'd often find that the oven still had its plastic wrapping on it. It had never been used! So even when people do have an oven, it's not their cooking method of choice when they are camping.

A lot of the people I meet at shows tell me that they love making meals in their slow-cooker when they are camping. You can prep your meal in the morning, and it will be ready for you when you get back to your site in the evening. There are other gadgets for this style of cooking as well such as the Instantpot (which everybody raves about) and the Remorska but do check that your leisure battery set-up can handle these if you are not on hook-up.

What sort of Kitchen Kit will you need?

Once you have decided how much 'normal' cooking you want to do when you are away in your campervan you will then have an idea of what sort of kitchen kit you will need to have in the van. As I like to cook properly while we are away, I sort of have a scaled-down duplicate set of the kitchen kit I have in my home kitchen. Often, if I find a new gadget that I really like, say a potato peeler, I buy two of them and keep one in the van. In my opinion you really do want to have a complete set of cooking equipment that stays in the van and not one that you have to think about packing every time. I sometimes do cooking demos at shows and there was one awful time when I forgot to put the saucepan I needed into the van as I liked to use it in the house as well. Now I have a duplicate that stays in the van!

So, before you choose your campervan check out the cooking facilities and how they will work with your style of cooking and in all weathers. With some smaller van designs you are literally cooking with your head in the pop-top and your nose about 6 inches from the wall which is something that really doesn't work for me but I recognise that for some people this is not an issue. Personally, I don't like cooking in the van at all (smells and condensation) but sometimes it is necessary in bad weather although, if the weather was that bad we'd probably eat in the pub or just make a soup'n'sarnie (toasted sandwich with a bowl of soup - love it!). When we had our Toyota Previa, which had a rear kitchen, I would really enjoy cooking under the tailgate and I am thinking of making a magnetic sun/rain shade to fix over the open back doors in our Vivaro where I can cook if we don't have the awning up.

If you are converting a van to get Motor Caravan status with DVLA your campervan will either need to have a fixed, two-ring gas/electric cooker or a fixed microwave in the van.

10. The Dining Area

In a perfect world, the weather would always be great when we are out camping and we would always be able to sit outside next to our van and eat our meals. There is nothing quite like waking up in the morning, stepping outside the van to a great view (preferably the beach in my case) then cooking and eating your full-English breakfast. Oohh, the smell of bacon cooking in the outdoors is hard to beat. Or sitting next to the van chatting with other campervan-friends and having a barbeque on a warm, gentle summer's evening. But real life just isn't like that (especially if you live in the UK) so you are going to need somewhere to sit in the van to eat you meals when the weather isn't so good. What sort of dining area you have is very dependent on the size of your van but your dining zone will need a table and some kind of seating and there are so many ways to create this in a campervan.

What sort of dining area you have really depends a lot on the size of your van. If you have a large motorhome you will probably have a dedicated dining booth somewhere in the van but for smaller vans the bed usually becomes the dining area in the daytime.

Dining Seating

When the van is in day mode, the seats for your diner are usually the rock & roll bed or the side bench seats of the bed. Some vans have front seats that can swivel around to the back (known as a captain's chair) and these seats then become part of the lounge/dining area when the van is static.

Swivel seats are a great idea, especially if you have a smaller van, and the swivel mechanism is relatively inexpensive and easy to fit if the van you are looking at doesn't already have them and you think that you would like to have them. You don't have to swivel both chairs, many vans just have a captain's chair for the passenger seat. Obviously, you won't be able to have captain's chairs if your kitchen zone is right next to the side door as the kitchen unit will cut off the front cab from the rear load area. But I have seen swivel chairs work well in a van that has a side kitchen.

The Table

The dining table is often a removable table that will have a centre 'leg' that screws into a hole in the floor or one that will attach, temporarily, to a bar on the wall. Either way, you will need to find a place to store the table when it is not being used. If your captain's chairs form part of your dining zone you may find that they are positioned so that they do not reach the dining table in a comfortable way and you can buy tables that swivel out on an arm that is fixed to the wall. These are usually produced by companies that supply the boating world and the tables made by Lagun are perfect for this although not cheap. I am also looking in to how it might be possible to fit individual tables to a captain's chair that fix on to the arm a bit like the writing tablets that you sometimes see on conference chairs.

I like to write on my laptop in our campervan, so we designed the dining table to also work as a computer workstation. I've had some inspiring moments when I am working on the laptop and looking out of the campervan window at a gorgeous beach view!

So if you think you may need to work in your van too you might want to consider this factor when you are thinking about a dining table and also if you can easily plug in to an electric socket while you are working if you need to keep charging as you go along.

If you are converting a van to get Motorhome Caravan status with DVLA, your table and seating will need to comply with their regulations. This is what they say on the GOV.UK website

https://www.gov.uk/government/publications/registering-a-diy-caravan/converting-a-vehicle-into-a-motorhome#dft-definition-of-motor-caravan

"The seats and table are required to be an integral part of the living accommodation area, and mounted independently of other items. The table must be capable of being mounted directly to the vehicle floor and / or side wall. The table mounting arrangement must be secured as a permanent feature, (bolted, riveted, screwed or welded), although the table may be detachable.

Permanently secured seating must be available for use at the table. The seats must be secured directly to the vehicle floor and / or side wall. The seats must be secured as a permanent feature (bolted riveted, screwed or welded)."

11. The Bathroom

A dedicated bathroom (usually a shower cubicle) is a bit of a luxury in a campervan but, I think, preferable if you are going away for long periods of time or wild camping a lot.

You will really need to have one of the larger vans to have a dedicated shower cubicle/ wet room which sometimes has the loo in it too and this often works really well. Bear in mind that you will need to have a larger water storage tank for this as well and if your tank is outside the van, the water may freeze if you are camping in colder climates or deep winter. If you want to have heated water, you will also need to have sufficient gas storage and space for the water heater.

Let's Talk Loos

OK, let's talk loos. In a smaller van, a proper toilet is not really an option but it can make a big difference to your camping life if you can have some sort of loo on board, especially if you wild camp. I'm afraid that there is no way to be delicate about this so let's dive in. Your toilet needs may be very different if there are just adults camping or if there are also children in your camping group. It may also become more critical if one of your group has an illness. Two of my friends went campervanning a lot when one of them had cancer and it did mean that the loo question became more important to them.

So, you will need to ponder on how your group specifically might need to use a loo while you are camping and make sure that everybody's needs are catered for. For us, it is really just about having a pee at night which makes it a lot easier to find a loo solution and there are lots of inexpensive portable loo options that you can buy and tuck away during the day. But do remember that you need to have the loo accessible at night when the bed is out.

There is then the question of disposal. Many portaloo toilets have a cassette-type design and you can remove the part with the contents and dispose of it when you get to a campsite in their disposal area. However, is you just need the loo for the occasional pee at night, then a lot of people use the bag/gel system in which you pee in to a disposal bag that has super-absorbent gel in it which absorbs the liquid and can be disposed of in the rubbish so there is not the bucket-walk in the morning. Some people say that cat litter in the bag works just as well.

If you need the loo for something more substantial that liquids, then it really is best to go down the proper, cassette loo route.

12. The Lounge

In a house, the lounge is usually where we relax in the evenings, so, for your van, you might want to think about how you want to relax in the evenings before you go to bed. Most of us vanners like to sit outside and have a nice meal and a glass of something and a chat before we go to bed but this obviously depends on the weather and if you are camping in places like Britain, warm evenings don't happen that often. This means you will need to think about how you would use the van inside on a colder evening or if you are stealth camping/staying at a pub overnight stop where you can't sit outside.

Glyn and I love using our time away to catch up on films and TV series on Netflix so our van is designed to be a very cosy 'cinema' in the evening. We pull out the bed, load it up with pillows/cushions/blankets and use a projector on to the white blind that we pull down at night between the cab and the back of the van. However, we watched films etc on our laptop when we were in Trev-the-Prev our Toyota Previa.

If you are going to put the van into night mode (bed down) in this way you may want to think about access to anything you might need and get what you need out before setting up the bed. Can you get to the clothes you need for the night? Can you get to any kitchen equipment if you are going to want a cup of tea or a snack? Can you get to the loo if you are not on a campsite with loos? Can you get to your electronics and/or plug them in for re-charge? After you have been camping in your van for a while you get into a routine and just do this automatically (most of the time!)

but it can be flippin' annoying if your sleeping t-shirt is under the bed or in a cupboard you can't now open.

Think it Through

If you prefer to sit and chat, watch TV or play board games then your dining area becomes your lounge. If you are a family, you may need to think how you can make this work with the number of people in relation to the seating area so, it you are viewing ready-made vans try and think through an evening inside the van if the weather is bad and you can't be outside at all. You may also need to think about how you are going to negotiate bed times if people want to go to sleep at different times as, unlike in a house, you can't just go upstairs to bed.

13. Storage

When you are living in a campervan, for even a few days, storage becomes very important as you need to store a lot of stuff in a very small space. Fortunately, campervanners have come up with some very clever ways to create storage in a campervan and I defy you to go on Pinterest and check out the storage ideas there without becoming addicted!

Obviously, every van is unique and the storage challenges will be very different in a micro camper to those in something like a high top, long length Iveco. Also, I have found that, naturally, different people have different priorities when it comes to storage - for some vanners their kitchen kit may be a priority while for others it may be their sports kit. As with all things campervan, it is a broad spectrum but, for me, there are five different types of storage in a van and these are:

- **Clothes storage**
- **Kitchen storage**
- **Bedding storage**
- **Outdoor Equipment storage**
- **Sports gear storage**

Let's look at them in detail.

Clothes Storage

Obviously, clothes storage depends a lot on the size of your van. Some vans even have mini wardrobes in them although, when we are camping, we don't tend to take clothes that will need to be hung up, but each to their own. When we had our Toyota Previa micro camper, we just had a strong, plastic storage box for our clothes and it seemed to work really well as it kept the clothes flat and damp-free. However, we knew that we wanted a bit more space in our Vivaro conversion so we adapted a small shelf unit to fit on to one side of the van so that the clothes are easily accessible.

The way you store your clothes tends to dictated by how many drawers or cupboards you have (if any). For me, I tend to think about our clothes being in six main categories;

- Undies
- Tops
- Bottoms
- Jackets
- Shoes
- Laundry

Undies

Maybe you have a dedicated draw for your undies (oohh fancy!) but, personally, I wouldn't want to give over such a valuable space to something that could easily be stored another way. I find that one of the best ways to store your fresh undies is in mesh bags. Obviously the size of the bags depends on your type of undies and how long you are going away for but you can buy bags of all different sizes quite cheaply on Amazon and eBay so you could even have a selection. I have bought a set of bags that are different colours, so our undies are even colour coded and we have our own bags. I separate my knickers from my socks and I have a purple bag for knickers and a blue bag for socks (possibly too much information) but it means that if you need to grab some fresh socks in the morning I know exactly where to go and, as you can partially see through the bag it's easy to get the exact pair of socks that you want that day. As these bags are soft so they can be squashed in to any space you like and you can be flexible if you need to use the hard spaces for something else that trip.

Tops

These can range from light t-shirts to really thick jumpers depending on the season you are camping although I would never go away without one thick jumper for the evenings. As I write this I am sitting in a coffee shop in Wales on one or our campervan trips and although it is the middle of June I am wearing a polo neck jumper as the weather has been freakily bad so do always have one serious jumper with you or at least several layers.

When I was in my twenties I did a lot of backpacking around the world and got used to getting as many clothes into a small space as possible and I found that rolling up items like T-shirts worked brilliantly. Not only does it give you maximum space it also keeps them relatively crease-free. You could then stack them (end-up so you can easily see which is which) in a canvas box at the bottom of a wardrobe if you are lucky enough to have one. You can do the same with light jumpers which lets you save your hanging space for jackets or longer/posher items like dresses. In our van we have created an 'open' shelf unit which is covered on 5 sides but has bungee elastic at the front and I can just reach in and get my t-shirts etc without having to open a door and I find that this works really well. We created it from an old wooden shoe rack!

I haven't done it myself, but I have heard of people storing larger jumpers in cushion covers so these items can also be used as a cushion too which sounds like a good idea.

Bottoms

These will mainly be jeans/trousers/shorts/skirts and some of these could be rolled up in the same way as the tops and stored in draws/boxes at the bottom of the wardrobe or wherever you are lucky enough to have such space.

Jackets

As these are generally bulky items hanging them up in the wardrobe is the best solution if you have one but of course you can't do this when they are wet. We have stretched a couple of bungee straps across the roof at the back of the van where we can hang wet clothes/towels so that they can dry when we are driving which works really well. Otherwise wall hooks are good if you have the height/space for these or we sometimes just put ours on the third front seat (if they are dry).

Shoes

These can be a bit tricky as they are quite bulky, and they can get wet and dirty. Probably having a plastic box for the shoes is the best solution which could go in the bottom of the wardrobe or in a large, under-bed drawer if you have one. We like to keep one slip-on pair each by the side door - I have some plastic, gardening-type crocs which are great even when it's wet. We can easily take them on and off for going in and out and I have seen people store their shoes vertically inside some bungee elastic stretched across a kitchen cupboard upright surface next to the side door.

Laundry

As your trip goes on you will be generating laundry and this needs to be stored somewhere, too. It is important that laundry is stored in a breathable container, so it is best to avoid plastic unless it is highly vented. I have found that our mesh bags work well for this too although you will need a larger laundry bag if you are going away for longer. You might also want to make sure that the laundry bag is not too near the head of the bed as you don't really want to be smelling dirty clothes all night!

Kitchen Storage

For me, there are five types of kitchen storage that you will need to think about:

- Saucepans, crockery and cutlery
- Larder Items
- Fresh Food (Not in Fridge)
- Fridge Food
- Cooker/Stove

Saucepans, Crockery and Cutlery

The first thing you need to think about before deciding where to store these items is do you mostly cook outside or inside? We cook outside mostly whether that is completely outside or in the awning as I loathe cooking inside, not only because of the smells but I just don't like being cramped when I cook. If you have a large, high-top van like a Sprinter this will not be an issue but I just love cooking outside unless it is a kettle for a cup of tea or something like beans on toast.

As we cook outside I like to have all my kit in one plastic storage box so I have the option to lift it outside and I then have everything with me and don't have to keep climbing in and out of the van. I sub-divide the box so that it is easier to find things e.g. a cutlery section. Of course, you may prefer to have these items in a drawer or cupboard if you have these facilities in your van.

You are also going to need to store your cooking/eating utensils and food inside the van. Your cooking utensils will include: saucepans and frying pans, plates/dishes/cups/glasses, cutlery, t82upperware, gadgets such as tin openers/bottle openers/graters/tongs (a lot depends on your style of cooking of course). You may have enough space to put these all in a cupboard or drawer but I keep mine all in a large plastic storage box which works best for me as I can lift the whole thing out if I am cooking outside and don't have to keep going in and out of the van to get them if they are all stored inside.

Larder Items

This includes things like: spices, rice, pasta, sauces, salt & pepper, jams, and tinned food. If you have space, you may want to dedicate a small area to these. As you don't need to access these items so frequently it is quite useful to have them in a cupboard or shelf in the van but I like to keep mine in a (yes, you've guessed it) plastic storage box so that I can grab it and take it all outside when I am cooking.

If you go on Pinterest, you'll find lots of ways to store these items. Bear in mind that, if they are stored in a shelf, they will need to be secure when the van is moving.

Fresh Food (Not in fridge)

This will mostly be items like fruit and veg. Again, I like to keep these in a ventilated box so that I can lift them in and out of the van. Some vanners with bigger vans like to keep their fruit in a small, net hammock that they hang under the units.

Fridge Food

Obviously, you will keep things like dairy, meat, salad, juices in your fridge or cool box. A proper campervan 3-way fridge can cost a lot of money. Waeco or Dometic, which are excellent camping fridges, can cost anything from £300 - £800 but, if you are spending weeks/months out camping would be really worth it. A 3-way fridge is one that can work on gas, mains electric and 12V electric (battery) so it means that you can keep it operating whether you are on hook-up, travelling or going wild. Because we are camping for mainly weekends or a week at this point in our lives, we have chosen a 2-way high-level cool box (these can cost from around £50 - £200) which can work on hook-up or 12V electrics (battery) and it is portable so we can take it out of the van if we want to.

However, remember that a cool box does not actually cool the interior in the same way as a proper compressor fridge does, the fan simply moves the cold air created by freezer blocks around the inside of the box. So, to keep the cool box cool, you will need to keep re-freezing the freezer blocks and many campsites have a freezer onsite that you can use but don't forget to mark your freezer blocks with a permanent marker so that you and other people will know which blocks are yours. Some people also freeze their milk/meat etc before they leave home and let these defrost in the box too to add to the cooling factor.

You will also need to consider what size of fridge/cool box you will need and/or have room for. Camping fridges are sized in internal litres and most cool boxes/fridges tend to run from 24 litres up to around 50 litres. You will need to think carefully how you access your fridge/cool box. Most fridges open sideways (although you can buy some that open at the top) and most cool boxes are top loaders. Questions to ask yourself are: can I get to the fridge when the van is in night mode, can I take the cool box out of the van if I want to, what capacity of fridge do I really need?

Again, just consider which fridge arrangement works best for your budget and your style of cooking and camping.

The Cooker/Stove

Before you can know what type of cooker you are going to need, you will need to ask yourself what sort of cooking do you intend to do in your campervan. Will you mostly eat out and just do simple snacks in the van or do you want to, pretty much, have a cooker like you have home (or something in between)? To one lady I met, her cooker needed to be a 4-ring full-facility stove as her meals were very important to her. She had had cancer and nutrition had saved her life so, for her, every meal was vital. So, she cooked in the van all the time and, as the cooker was built in, there was no need to store another cooker.

Most people like to have some sort of outdoor cooking kit and this is usually a gas cooker and/or barbeque set. Can you manage with a single gas cooker that runs on canisters or do you need something more substantial like a double gas-cooker running off of a refillable gas cylinder with a regulator? If you use a refillable gas cylinder then you will need to consider safe storage for it in the van which usually involves a proper cupboard and safety straps.

Personally, I am not keen to have a gas cylinder in the van and with my style of cooking I don't really need anything that substantial anyway. One day when I was travelling along the M4 motorway the traffic came to a standstill for around half an hour because of an accident. Once it was cleared and we were able to drive on again, I saw one of the older style VW campervans on the hard shoulder which had been completely gutted by fire. Apparently, the gas cylinder had caused it. Of course, most gas cylinders are totally fine and I do appreciate that if you are camping for long periods they do make sense but please do everything that you can to make sure that your installation is safe.

If you camp on electric hook-up most of the time, then you might want to consider an electric cooker of some kind.

We have a portable induction hob inside the van, and we love it! It boils the kettle in no time, it is safe as there is no flame and it doesn't get hot except under the pan and I always think that, if you are paying for hook-up, you may as well make the most of it and save your gas. One of the members of our converters group uses a Teppanyaki grill (£30-£40) to cook on (it's like a long hotplate) but you are going to need some sort of table/kitchen unit to put this on when you are cooking.

However, you may want additional cooking facilities depending on your van, camping style and budget, like a remorska, a slow cooker or a Cadac Safari. However, you often need less than you think (unless you are living in your van) and it was my desire to create lots of nutritious, one-ring meals that led me to writing my books and blog as The Camper Cookie.

If you are going to cook outside a lot, you will also need some sort of foldout camping kitchen. In this case you will need to be able to store the camping kitchen when it is folded up and usually the garage is the best place for this.

Outdoor Equipment Storage

This is all the bigger stuff that you need to carry such as: awning, chairs, tables, groundsheets, cooking kit, storage units and, if you are sporty, there may be sports kit too. Naturally these will all fold down but they still need a lot of space in the van and may often need to be stored when they are a bit mucky or wet so bear that in mind too. A lot of campervans have a 'garage' area at the back which is a larger space under the seating/bed where these items can slide in. So, think about what large items you will need to store and how you are going to access them when you are choosing your van.

As these larger items will usually all have to bundle in to one space, you might want to think about the order that you load them so that you can get to what you need easily at the other end. This is not so critical if you are going to download onto a campsite, but if you are going wild or stealth camping you may, say, just want to get the chairs out so you will need to load these last so that you don't have to unpack all the other large items to get to them. I would also suggest that if you are going to arrive somewhere late and go straight to bed that you set the van in night mode as much as you can before you leave so that you are not struggling in the dark and possibly rain to change the van before you can sleep in it. After a while you will develop your own system for loading which people tend to refine as they go along.

Sports Gear Storage

This is probably going to be things like: cycle gear, wetsuit, walking gear, riding gear, climbing gear etc and, depending on your sport, you will really have to think about this when you are choosing/designing a van. Bear in mind that this type of kit often has to come into the van when it is wet and dirty so having somewhere to hang it or putting it in the garage is probably best. Or, you might consider having some sort of outside storage for it like a back box or a roof box.

14. The Awning

When you go camping in a micro to medium campervan, having an awning can make a big difference to your camping experience and most campervanners do take an awning of some kind with them. An awning is defined as a closable tent intended to be fixed to a stationary vehicle or to stand free of the vehicle.

There are many different types of awning and what you choose depends a lot on your camping style and budget. If you are wild camping or stealth camping a lot you will not be using an awning much and maybe you just want to invest in a tarp of some kind that can provide a bit of shelter when the situation allows it but can be put up and taken down easily.

However, if you do camp on campsites then you want to consider something more substantial. And, sometimes, having a large enough driveaway awning may mean that you can manage with a smaller campervan which may open up a larger range of van models for you to choose from. An awning also marks your pitch so that, hopefully, you don't drive back to the campsite and find that somebody else has set-up on your pitch (although this did happen to us once despite our awning being there!).

But before you buy an awning (which can be a considerable investment as £400-£500 for a new awning is around average price!) you need to be clear about your requirements and your priorities as there are a lot of different designs to choose from and you want to get it right.

There are eight things you need to consider before you buy an awning:

- Your camping frequency
- Size of awning and vehicle
- Type of awning
- How is it going to attach to your vehicle?
- Does it have a groundsheet?
- How easy is it to put up and down?
- Do you want people to sleep in it?
- How many openings do you want?

Your Camping Frequency

Are you the sort of family who likes to go to one campsite for a week and stay there and explore from that as a base or are you a couple who likes to move on to a different campsite every couple of days and maybe wild camp in between? If you are the family, then you probably want a more substantial awning that can comfortably fit four people sitting and eating and is easy to cook in. It also won't matter to you if it takes quite a bit of time and effort to put it up and take it down as you will only be doing that once in the week. If you tend to meet up with friends or other families you might want to consider something that works well between two vans/tents and maybe even a larger gazebo/shelter might work best for you.

However, if you are the couple, then you will want something a bit smaller that goes up and down very quickly and easily. It is also likely to be essential that it is a driveaway awning as well.

Size of Awning and Vehicle

The size of awning you choose will depend on how many people are in the camping group and whether you want it to act a bit like an extra tent for some of your co-travellers to sleep in. If you are very tall you might also want to check out the height of the awning before you buy it as many of them are around 190cm (6ft 2ins) at their highest point which is going to be annoying if you are that height or taller. However, many of the awning ranges come in different heights but you will need to make sure that the taller ones will fit your van. Most VW Transporter-type vans are around 190cm high which means that your awning will need to be round about this height too. High top vans tend to be around 246cm and many awning ranges have awnings in that height as part of their range. The connecting flaps on a lot of awnings will go a bit higher than the awning to reach the top of the van but you may find that the 'join' is not so good or weatherproof.

You will also need to consider how big and how heavy the awning is when it is packed up as you will need to find storage space for it in the van and awnings can take up a significant amount of space in a smaller campervan.

Types of Awning

The first question you need to ask yourself is - do you want a porch awning, a driveaway awning or a standalone awning? A driveaway awning lets you detach the part of the awning that connects to the van and then zip up the awning like a tent. The major advantage of this is that you can store a lot of your equipment in the awning (e.g. cooker, chairs, tables etc) which means you don't have to pack everything up into the van when you want to go out for the day. It also gives you a lot more door-privacy. However, if this is not important to you, you may just want a tarp or a sunblind that pulls out from the side of the van which gives you a bit of shade and rain shelter over the door. Or you may want a separate gazebo/shelter that is virtually a roof on legs with the option of having side walls if you want it.

You may also want to consider a rear awning as some people like to have their awning over the barn doors or tailgate at the back of the van and, if you are camping in a micro camper, this may be the only option.

How will it attach to your Van?

If you are going to choose an awning that joins to the van, then you need to consider how it will attach to the van. If you just have a sunblind awning, then it will pull out or wind out from the holder that is fixed to the side of the vehicle. Some awnings can be 'fed' into a metal channel that is fixed to the side of the van and then pegged down with guy ropes. Others may be held on the van by magnets, attached to roof bars or have guy ropes that are thrown over the van and pegged down on the other side.

Does it Have a Groundsheet?

Awnings can come with no groundsheet, a zip-in/clip-in groundsheet or a sewn-in groundsheet. There are pros and cons to all of these, and you just need to decide what meets your requirements. Our current awning doesn't have a groundsheet, so we have a separate one that covers the front half of the awning where we enter which has worked well for us. Having a separate groundsheet can certainly make packing up easier if the ground is wet as you can handle the wet groundsheet separately from the awning. Some awnings come with a clip-in or zip-in groundsheet so that you have the option of having it in the awning or not and maybe this is the most flexible option. Other awnings have a sewn-in groundsheet which can be a bit of a pain to sweep out but is nicer in bad weather. Some campsites insist that your groundsheet is breathable to preserve their grass so do check if your sewn-in groundsheet is breathable or not.

How Easy is it to Put Up and Down?

For us, this is one of the most important factors when choosing an awning. We really didn't want an awning that felt like we were putting up a tent but, for some people who are staying put for the week, this is not an issue. There are really three main types of support mechanisms when it comes to awnings at the moment : poles, air beams and pop-up. With an awning that is supported by poles, you erect it in much the same way as you would with a tent - feeding poles through slots and pushing them in to retainers at the bottom. With this kind of awning it can make a big difference as to how many people are available to help with the operation.

The other, more recent, type of support mechanism for an awning is air beams. In this type, the supporting 'beams' are created by inflating them with air from an air pump. They go up and come down very quickly and work very well so long as you don't get a puncture in your air beam. Their only real disadvantage is price at the moment, but I think that they will probably become more affordable in time.

There are also a few pop-up awnings which literally pop-up in seconds and you then just peg them down (we loved our Quechua Base Seconds pop-up awning). These tend to be the smaller awnings or utility tents, but they work well if there are not too any people in the camping group. They can be a bit difficult to twist down into their flat shape and to get them back in their bag, but you do get used to it with practise.

Do You Want People to Sleep in it?

Some campervanners use their awning as an extra bedroom so that they can take friends/children in their van if it only sleeps two people. For some awnings you can buy fabric, inner 'rooms' that you can just hook up to attachments inside the awning and these can work well as extra bedrooms.

How Many Openings Do You Want?

This may sound like a minor thing, but it can make a big difference to your camping experience if you like to sit by the van a lot. Do you want a lot of privacy or do you want an awning that is brighter and has more windows/doors to give it a more open feeling? Do you want to be able to open up the side in front of the van door so that you can have an open view, maybe with the fabric making a sunblind top for shade? Do you want the option to orientate your awning in different directions but still have access to the van door? Do you want plastic windows or windows that can be rolled down to give fresh air but still have insect mesh so that you don't get lots of unwanted creatures in the awning? When you choose an awning, it might be worth going through this list and mentally trying out these different scenarios.

Her are some of the main brands of awning you might like to check out:

Movelite T range, Sheltapod, Olpro Breeze, Decathlon range, Outwell, Vango, Kampa Travel Pod range, Khyam, Zempire.

15. Electrical Power

For most people, having some sort of electrical power in their campervan is a must. When you are away you will probably want to run devices like: lights, TV, space heater, water heater, hair dryer, fridge, kettle, induction hob, microwave oven, vent fan or phone/tablet/laptop charger. Not everybody has all of these appliances but, chances are, you will have some of them.

I am not a technical expert on electrically wiring a campervan although I have had to learn the basics along the way and, if you are going to be a campervan owner, I think it is a good idea to, at least, have an appreciation of how the different electrical systems work in a campervan. This will also help you check that any van you buy can give you the electrical power that you need or how you can install extra if it doesn't already have it.

Main Types of Electrical Supply

There are four main ways that you can bring electrical power into your van:

- **Mains Hook-up**
- **12V Leisure Battery**
- **Solar Power**
- **Diesel Generator**

Let's take a look at these individually now.

- **Mains Hook-up**

This is when you plug your van in to the 240V AC (Alternating Current) mains electric system (sometimes called shore power) and you will need to be on a campsite that provides pitches with hook-up to be able to do this. You'll usually pay a little bit more per night for hook-up (around £3-£5) and you can use as much electricity as you like for that fee. This becomes more relevant if you are camping on a cold night and want to keep an electric heater on all night so then you do really get value for money. It is also one of the reasons that we have a portable induction hob in our campervan as why use up your gas for cooking when you have paid for electricity (and induction hobs are brilliant in a campervan anyway).

If you are going to buy a ready-made campervan then you will probably already have the hook-up facility installed in the van which lets you plug your appliances into normal electrical sockets in the van much like you do at home. You'll see a covered inlet socket on the side of the van where you plug the connection cable into the vehicle and the other end of this cable will plug in to the site's hook-up bollard. Campsite electrics tend to run at a lower current rating than a house (a house is 20A and most sites are 16A or 10A) so you do have to be a bit careful about the demand that you put on their circuit. If you do overload their circuit, you will trip the MCB (miniature circuit breaker) that is in the bollard a bit like tripping a fuse at home. It's not the end of the world but, understandably, the campsites don't like it.

You can buy connection cables that have a safety power breaker on the cable which will temporarily cut off the electricity if there is a problem and it is a good idea to have one of these to protect any nasty electricity spikes coming in to your van and frying your electrics. Most connection cables are 25 metres long and you do really want this as a minimum.

To make sure that you are not going to overload your hook-up connection, it is a good idea to have a general idea of how much current typical appliances pull off of the system. Here's a table that shows the wattage and amps demands of typical appliances:

Appliance	Power(W)	Current(A)
Domestic kettle	2,000	8.7
Iron	1,300	5.6
Camping kettle	750	3.3
Microwave oven 800W cooking power	1,000	4.4
Domestic fan heater 1kW	1,000	4.4
Water heater	850	3.7
Camping fan heater	750	3.3
LCD TV	45	0.2
Refrigerator	135	0.6
Battery charger	100	0.4
Hair dryer	1500	5.2
Toaster	900	3.9

In my experience, the main appliances you have to be careful with are domestic kettles, heaters and hair dryers as these make a high demand on the electrical power. Fortunately, you can buy low wattage kettles, travel irons and mini hair dryers that are especially designed for travelling and that don't cause a problem. (When we had our micro camper, the Toyota Previa, I would sometimes use my mini hair dryer as a heater for the space first thing in the morning when a van can feel a little cool and damp. I could hang it up on a hook and it worked brilliantly as it had the space feeling warm in no time, just enough to make getting out of bed not too traumatic.)

Also, remember that, if you are using more than one appliance it will all add up and you could reach an over-demand situation without realising it. However, for most normal camping situations you should be alright.

- **12V Leisure Battery**

One of the joys of owning a campervan is that you can park up in beautiful, remote places and sometimes spend the night there too, known as 'going wild'. In this case you are not going to have any mains hook-up and you will have to rely on a leisure battery. A leisure battery provides 12V DC (Direct Current) power to the living space and it looks pretty much like the car battery that starts your vehicle. They come in different Ah (amp Hour) ratings, which tells you how much current the battery can deliver over how much time, and ideally you want one of at least 100Ah.

The difference between a leisure battery and a vehicle (starter) battery is that the starter battery is designed to deliver a big surge of energy to start the engine whereas a leisure battery is designed to give you smaller currents over a longer period of time. Leisure batteries can also tolerate being partially discharged (although you don't want to discharge your leisure battery fully as this damages it) whereas a starter battery will not tolerate deep cycling.

You do need to think of your 12V system as a completely different electrical network to your 240V AC system as appliances that work on the mains AC system will not work directly off of a 12V battery. However, you can buy a piece of kit called an inverter which will allow you to plug normal, household appliances with a regular plug in to the 12V system. An inverter is basically a box with a 12V plug at one end (like the one that would plug in to your cigarette lighter socket in a car) and a normal household-type socket at the other end where you could plug in your, say, laptop. However, appliances that pull a lot of electricity (like hair dryers, toasters) will very rapidly drain a leisure battery so you do need to think carefully about what you plug in to an inverter.

You can buy electrical appliances that are specially adapted to plug in to the 12V system, (like TVs, water pump, sound system) and the control panel on many 12V systems often has a USB charger socket on it so it is great for charging phones/tablets etc. Camping fridges are often able to work on both mains AC electric and 12V electric and are known as 2-way fridges (you can also get 3-way fridges that will work on gas as well). Where the 12V system is particularly valuable is in powering the lighting in the van as LED lights pull very little power and there are lots of gorgeous, lighting fittings that are designed for 12V.

The general consensus among campervan self-build converters is that you really need more than one leisure battery (unless you are going to spend all of your time on campsite with hook-up) and most converters have 2 or sometimes 3 batteries wired in parallel in their vans.

Leisure batteries can be topped up with charge by either the mains hook-up, current coming from the vehicle battery when you are driving (make sure that you have a split charger between the vehicle battery and the leisure battery) or by solar power from solar panels fitted on the roof of the van. Sometimes all three.

- **Solar Power**

Unless you are going to spend all of your camping trips on campsites with hook-up, it is really worth considering getting a campervan with some solar power or consider installing some in the van you buy or choose to convert.

There are 2 ways to bring solar power into your van: through a *fixed system* or through a *portable system.*

The Fixed Solar Energy System

This is where you permanently fix a photo voltaic (PV) solar panel(s) to the roof of your van in much the same way that you would if you fitted solar panels to your house. Basically, wires from the solar panel are run down through the body of the van and go to a solar charge controller unit. This is usually a small 'box' that has a digital display showing the voltage /charge and then another set of wires run from the controller unit to the leisure battery. In this way electrical current generated in the solar panels can run safely to charge up your leisure battery. You can buy complete kits that include the panel/controller/wires and fixings but it is best to make sure that your controller is able to both regulate the current (make sure that the panels don't overload your battery) and has a diode which means that the flow of electricity can only go one way - from the panels to your leisure battery, so it won't drain the battery at night.

You can now buy 2 types of fixed solar panels: crystalline and thin film. Crystalline panels are the rigid ones like the ones you see on houses and thin film panels are, like they say, much thinner and are made of flexible material. Thin film panels are sometimes cheaper than the crystalline panels but tend to be less efficient and you do need to make sure that they are firmly attached to the roof so that the wind cannot lift them while you are driving down the motorway. However, if you want a lighter, slimmer profile on the top of the van they are ideal for this. The rigid panels are heavier and will need to be fixed to the roof of the van via something more substantial that usually involves drilling into the van roof. Some campervans now have solar panels that can tilt upwards so that they can follow the direction of the sun to get maximum charge.

The Portable Solar Energy System

A portable solar panel can range from something small, like the size of a book and this can even be attached to your backpack while you are out hiking, through to a large, solid panel like the ones that go on the roof, but it can be propped up on the ground next to the van. Some are in the middle and are known as briefcase solar panels as they look a bit like a briefcase when they are folded up. The advantages of having a portable solar panel is that you don't need to drill holes in the van and they can be moved to follow the sun. They attach to the battery by crocodile clips, but I would still want a charge controller between my portable panel and leisure battery to be on the safe side. The disadvantage is that you can really only use it when you are stationary whereas panels fitted to the roof are working all the time but, their disadvantage is that they will not work well if you have to park in the shade.

But what size (wattage) solar panel do you need? This is a bit like asking how long is a piece of string and depends on how many appliances you have running off of your leisure battery, their rating and for how long you need to use them each day. Obviously, it will also depend on the seasons you go camping in (winter, summer or both) and the general conditions you are parking in as, naturally, a solar panel is less efficient in low-sun conditions. (*Note: surprisingly, solar panels can become less efficient in situations of intense sun too - they tend to have an optimum range somewhere in the middle*)

If you are inclined, you can calculate the exact load that you will be putting on your battery system and this will give you a good indication of what wattage solar panel or panels you will need to meet your general power needs. You will need to know the power that is pulled by each appliance you have and how long you will want to run it each day and I suggest you Google something like "How to Calculate Wattage for Solar Panel for Campervan' and this will walk you through the calculations. However, for those that want an overview here is a general guideline.

For a small Campervan with a 110 Ah Leisure Battery (spring to autumn):

A 60W solar panel will power lights, water pump, radio and TV for 2 hours per day

An 85W solar panel will power lights, water pump, radio and TV for 3 hours per day plus some 240V appliances

A 100W solar panel will power lights, water pump, radio and TV for 5 hours per day plus some 240V appliances

Most self-build converters say that you if you are going to install solar panels then 100W is the minimum and most choose to go 200-300W for their installation which can be achieved with one or more panels.

- **Diesel Generator**

The main advantage of a portable diesel generator is that it can give you relatively cheap power if you camp off grid a lot. However, they are generally noisy and will disturb your neighbours if you are parked near people and most campsites do not allow them, understandably.

Cheaper generators may also cause electrical spikes or surges in voltage that can result in damage to your campervan's sensitive electronic control systems so it is better to invest in a generator with the technology to provide a surge-free electrical supply. Most portable diesel generators will cost between £300 and £1,000.

Of course, a generator must always be used outside because of the danger from exhaust and carbon monoxide. Always place it downwind and make sure the fumes do not go directly into yours or other people's vans. You will also need to shield it from rain while still making sure that it is ventilated.

16. Heating

For me, part of the joy of camping is that you are more in contact with nature and the elements and I quite enjoy being aware of the natural temperature. However, there are times when you do really want some heating in your camper, especially if you go camping in the winter as well as the summer.

There are two different scenarios when it comes to heating your van: when you are on *hook-up* and when you are *not on hook-up*.

Heating When You Are on Hook-Up

This is the easy scenario as, basically, you can plug in any heater that you would normally plug in at home into your van 240V system. As you are probably paying a flat fee for hook-up (£3-£5 per night is common) then you may as well make the most of that electrical supply. What sort and size of heater depends a lot on the size of your van, a large Sprinter van is going to need a lot more heating than a VW Transporter and, remember, heat rises so in a high top vehicle a lot of the heat will be up near the roof (unless you use a far infrared heater). If your van is well insulated, then you won't need a lot of heat to get the interior to a comfortable temperature so do first maximise your insulation before focusing on the heating kit.

As well as making sure that you have insulated the walls well if you are doing a self-build conversion, you want to make sure that you have insulation for the side/back windows and the cab as this is where most of the heat loss happens.

Most campervan side/back windows have some sort of fabric curtains which are pulled across when it gets dark but, in my experience, these will not really provide much insulation on a cold night. You can sometimes buy thermal blinds which are ready-made for some types of van but you might need to think about making a thermal blind yourself if you cannot find ones to fit your windows. You can buy thermal blind material online by the metre which is quilted and has a silver radiant barrier on one side to reflect the heat. You can fix them to the window with flexible, plastic suckers.

When it comes to insulating the cab windows, again you can buy complete sets that cover all the cab windows but these often cost somewhere between £60 and £100 though it might be worth it if you have a captain's chair and use the cab space at night. If you don't, then often having a pair of thermal curtains pulled across to isolate the cab from the back will do the trick.

Here are some of the heaters you might consider using when you are on Hook-up:

- **Fan Heaters**
  There are many portable fan heaters that you can plug in to the sockets and these will heat up and dry out the space quickly which is great for early morning or when you are going to bed. However, they are noisy and I personally wouldn't want one on all night. For safety, try and make sure that you get one that automatically cuts out if it falls over. The latest technology in fan heaters uses ceramic heating discs to create the heat rather than a resistive wire so are considered safer.

- **Far Infrared Heaters**
  These are a relatively new idea and more and more people are using these in their houses, workshop, studios now as, not only do they produce a nice even heat, they are cheap to run, look great and they also keep down damp so prevent mould. Most of them are a square radiating panel that looks like a picture you hang on the wall and they simply plug in to the mains. You can get them in all different sizes and wattage, and you need to select the right one for the volume of the space you are going to heat.

  Far infrared radiation acts a bit like the warmth we get from the sun, so it is healthy as well as comfortable. It doesn't heat the air like a fan heater would (causing the heat to rise to the top of the van), it heats objects (including yourself) so you feel that nice gentle heat that you would feel if you were sitting sunbathing. The panels get warm, but they are not dangerous to touch. We have one in our van and, if it is a very cool night, we leave it on all night on a thermostat so that the temperature never really drops but is comfortable for sleeping. One of their main advantages is that they are also completely silent. You will pay around £100-£250 for a panel that is a good size for a van and one of its unique benefits is that you can install it on the ceiling if your head is not going to touch it as the heat will radiate downwards and not stay on the ceiling.

- **Oil-Filled Radiators**
  These look like a small radiator, but they are filled with oil instead of water the way a house radiator is. They are good for a small space, but their

disadvantage is that they take a while to come to temperature. However, they are safe and silent and could be used for background heat overnight on a thermostat socket. You can now buy a similar heater that is oil-free and has aluminium or ceramic inside instead which heats up a bit quicker than the oil-filled ones. The disadvantage can be the size and weight, but you can find some that are small enough for a campervan.

- **Convector Heater**
  Convector heaters use an exposed metal element in the base that quickly heats up and spreads warmth to the surrounding air. The warm air generated rises up through the heater grill and circulates around the room, creating a convection current that will heat up the space. They are lightweight and heat the space up quickly. They are also quiet except for the occasional click as they switch on and off to keep the room at the temperature on the setting which you can select on the controls on the side.

Heating When You Are *Not* on Hook-up

When you don't have mains electrical supply you will need to look to another type of fuel to create heat in your campervan.

- **Diesel Heaters**

With diesel heaters, air is sucked in from outside of the vehicle into a combustion chamber where it's mixed with diesel and ignited to heat up a heat exchanger. The exhaust gases are vented to the outside through an exhaust pipe. An internal 12V fan sucks air from inside the vehicle over the heat exchanger, which warms it up, and then blows it back into the interior of the vehicle. The main advantage is that the heater draws fuel from your vehicle's existing diesel fuel tank. This means that you already have one very large fuel supply, so you don't need to worry about carrying and sourcing an additional fuel type. However, as it uses a fan, it will be noisy and you will need a good leisure battery preferably with some solar input. It is also important to make sure that it is properly maintained so that it doesn't create any fumes. You are probably going to have to pay somewhere between £500 and £2000 for the system and you will need to have somebody competent to install it as pipes have to pass through the floor of the van and you want to make sure it is safe.. The main brands are Eberspacher and Webasto although there are some cheaper but good enough ones coming over from China now but do your research.

- **Gas (Propane) Heaters**

Propane-fuelled systems are similar to diesel systems but use gas as the fuel supply. This could be disposable canisters (inside the vehicle in a cupboard) or a refillable propane tank often underslung beneath the van. If you're already using propane tanks in your van, you may be able to tap into your existing propane lines. Propex seems to be the main brand.

- **Gas Cartridge Heaters**

These look a bit like an upright version of the portable camping gas cooker and use the small butane gas canisters and have piezo ignition (no matches needed). They are a much cheaper option but, you will need to be conscious of safety and fumes.

- **Woodburning Stove**

These look great and give the van a really cosy feeling with the advantage that this type of heat dries out the air as well as heating the space so it stops damp building up in the van. You can now buy mini burners especially designed for campervans and some you can even cook on as well. The fuel (wood) is relatively cheap and you may even be able to find some for free.

The disadvantages are that you will need a flue that passes through the roof of the van so they will make stealth camping very difficult. You also need to be conscious of safety as, obviously, they get very hot to touch and you do not want to catch it as you pass by and you do not want it near anything combustible, so do think carefully about where you site it in the van. However, you can buy insulated flues which helps from that point of view. Another disadvantage - somebody has to light it and clean it, but you may well enjoy that ritual.

17. Ventilation

A campervan is pretty much a large metal box on wheels which you cook, eat, sleep and relax in. Professional and self-build converters go to great lengths to insulate this box so that it is warm enough to be a lounge/bedroom at night. However, it also important to make sure that the space is well ventilated, not only to make it comfortable on a hot night, but also for air quality, especially if you have bathroom facilities in your van. There is also the issue of water vapour building up inside which can cause condensation - the mortal enemy of campervans. This vapour builds up not only from the bathroom or cooking, but also from people simply breathing in and out. So, it is a compromise between retaining warmth when necessary and getting enough cool, fresh air flow when necessary.

There are several ways to create coolness and fresh air in your van apart from the obvious such as opening windows and doors and they range from the fancy to the really simple.

- **Extractor Roof Vent**

Hot air rises so it makes sense to have some sort of outlet in the roof. The Rolls Royce of roof vents is an extractor vent with a fan that runs off of the 12V electrical supply to physically draw the stale air out or suck the fresh, cool air in. If you are converting your own van you will need to cut a square hole (around 14 inches) in the roof of the van to fit the vent and make sure that it is properly sealed as you don't want rain dripping in through the roof on a stormy night. There are many fan roof vents to choose from but it is good to buy one with an insect mesh as part of it as you don't want the nasty, bitey insects coming in and feasting on you in the night (what is the point of mosquitos?). If, like us, you like as much blackout in the van as possible at night or you do serious stealth camping, you will also need one with a blackout screen that can be pulled across or maybe you can just make one of your own.

- **Pop-Up Roof Vent**

This is basically a square, vent in the roof that you can pop-up to create a gap all round for air to flow in. It does not have a fan so you are just getting whatever air flow is generated by the outside conditions. They are usually waterproof and windproof and can be locked for security. This vent will also require a hole to be cut and sealed in the roof of the van.

- **Wind-Powered Roof Vent**

These look a bit like a large mushroom sitting on the roof of the van and have a non-electrical fan part that whirls around according to the wind speed outside, usually when you are driving. However, in some you can control the size of the opening in the vent so you can regulate the airflow although it will not be working on a still, muggy night while you are sleeping.

- **Solar Roof Vents**

These also look a bit like a mushroom on the roof although with a lower profile. They have a solar collector panel on the top which drives a small fan and on some you can choose to draw out or draw in air. They tend to be quite small and do not have the flow speed of a 12V electrical fan, but they are quiet. However, a bit like the solar lights in your garden, it won't last long at night.

- **Louvred air vents**

If you are happy to have some constant fresh air, you can have one or more, louvred air vents fitted in strategic positions in the walls of your campervan. Again, you'll need to cut holes in the side of the van where you want to fit the vents, but these vents are quite cheap so it is a low-cost option. Make sure you fit fly screens behind each vent to stop unwanted bugs getting into the van. If you like to camp a lot in Scotland or wet areas, you may want to make sure that the mesh has small enough holes to stop the midges as well as the mosquitos. Personally, I would also want to create some kind of removable covering that can stop the cold air coming in on a winter's night.

- **Wind Deflectors on Windows**

These are plastic strips that go over the top of side windows and I call them 'window eye-brows'. This means that you can leave the windows open a little at night without any rain coming in or anyone realising that the window is open from a security perspective. They don't create a lot of air flow, but every bit of fresh air intake counts when it comes to ventilating a campervan. You simply stick them on the van using 3M tape which sounds like it would be ripped off by the wind but ours have stayed on throughout our many travels.

- **Window Lattice/Mesh**

You can buy a plastic, fold up window lattice that opens out to fit the open top third of a side window which you jam in by raising the window to fit. This means that you can have a bigger air gap than the 'eye-brows' and I gather these are popular with dog-owners as you can leave the window partially open without any dogs escaping. I have also seen people create a similar item to fill in the open window space with a piece of rigid insect mesh and magnets.

- **Opening Rear Doors**

If it is a really warm night and we are parked somewhere safe, like on a campsite, we will just leave our rear, barn doors cracked with a bungee strap wrapped around the handles. We also have a mesh curtain that we can pull across the back which stops most bugs.

18. Entertainment

For most people, having entertainment facilities in the van is going to mean something electronic although there is a lot to be said for a good old-fashioned board game on a rainy day. For Glyn and I, one of the joys of being away in the campervan is being able to cosy-in once it's dark with a glass of Kraken (a totally gorgeous, spiced rum) and do a boxset binge, usually through Netflix/Prime. However, if you too want to watch/listen to something that needs electrical supply/Wi-Fi facilities, what are the options?

- **Television**

There are 2 routes that you can use to access television programs in a campervan and they are: through digital terrestrial TV with Freeview/aerial or satellite TV (such as Sky) using a dish receiver. For satellite in the UK, a 40-65cm dish should be OK but the further you get away from the UK, the larger the dish you will need in order to pick up channels like the BBC and ITV.

Obviously, you are going to need a television set and, ideally, you would want an LED television that can run on 240V mains electricity and 12V electricity and companies such as Avtex make these especially for the campervan/caravan market. Some of their dual supply TVs also have built-in Freeview HD, satellite tuner as well as a DVD player and you can even record your films/programs onto a stick drive and play it on the TV via a USB port. They also have one-button tuning which can be really helpful as you will need to re-tune your TV every time you arrive at a new location. These TVs are also said to have good viewing angle range and this is important in a van as you are often much closer and at a different angle to what you would be at home sitting on the sofa. Some even have an HDMI connector so that gaming consoles (PS4 and Xbox One) can run through them as well. These clever TVs will set you back somewhere around £400 but it may well be worth it for the convenience and quality.

If you are happy to have a TV that just runs off of the 12V supply, then you can buy one with the Freeview and satellite inside for around £200. A 12v TV draws only around 2-3amps per hour so it won't really impact your battery for a few hours viewing before re-charging and no problem at all if you are on solar power (although be aware of what else you are running at the same time, e.g. lights, fridge, phone charging).

If you just have a standard LED TV, you can always buy a separate Freeview box or satellite box and link it up by cable and these are not expensive now.

- **Laptop**

If you have a decent sized laptop you can of course use this to access subscription streaming such as Netflix/Prime/Now and catch-up TV like BBC iPlayer. The only problem you are likely to come across using this kit for viewing is the speed of the local Wi-Fi. Many campsites offer Wi-Fi, some are free, and some are paid, and you get charged something like £3 a day or £5 for three days although it can be considerably more on some sites. However, with so many people using it, the on-site Wi-Fi often doesn't have the capacity to stream video and you just get the buffering circle whizzing around or constant stalling. You can overcome this by getting a Wi-Fi Booster kit which will boost the campsite wireless signal and repeat it at full strength. This allows you to create your own secure wireless network in your campervan and share the boosted connection with all your devices.

If the campsite charges per device then you will save money as these Wi-Fi booster kits will only be seen once by the campsite router. These booster kits can run on mains 240V electric and 12V battery electric supply. These kits cost around £150.

However, if you really want to be more independent and have your own mobile hotspot then you can get a motorhome 4G Mobile Wi-Fi Kit which you use with any SIM card to create your hotspot. These kits let you share the internet connection with, typically, up to 5 devices - smartphones, tablets, iPads or computers. It has an external antenna booster which allows you to pick up even very faint mobile data signals and, because it is 4G, it is fast enough for streaming video. They sell for around £150.

To watch live television on your laptop computer you can buy a USB TV tuner. You plug the tuner in to a spare USB port on your computer and install the software, but it is important to check that your computer does have the correct operating system/system requirements before getting one. Please note that this is not an option for the iPad one, as it does not have USB ports. As the aerial inside the USB stick is very small, it may be necessary to buy an additional external aerial to boost the signal received.

On your laptop you can also watch pre-recorded programs/series that you download at home on your faster broadband before you come away. You can either download them directly to the laptop or have them on a (large capacity) stick drive that you plug in to a USB port. However, always check that the downloads are working before you leave home as we have settled down to watch a good, pre-recorded film only to find that it won't play which is a bit frustrating.

To really enjoy your viewing you might want to invest in a nano or pico projector and a portable or pull down screen which means you can sit inside or outside and have a cinema moment if it is not going to annoy any neighbours. To get anything decent you will need to spend upwards of £300 and make sure that you get one that is 'short fall' as, in the van, you are likely to be watching at close range.

- **Phone/Tablet**

Don't forget that there is lots of free entertainment that can be accessed by your phone or tablet although naturally this is more for personal viewing. There are mountains of video content on YouTube which includes some classic TV as well as videos on every subject under the sun so you could catch up on those 'How to Crochet' videos that you have been meaning to watch for a long time (only kidding...but who knows?). With the right cabling, you can also connect your tablet to your TV and play the videos through there for a wider audience.

If you are happy to just listen rather that view, there are enough podcasts to keep you entertained until the end of time. Apps like Castbox and Podbean are all free and again you can listen to anything from the silly to the sublime. If you are happy to pay a subscription, then submerging yourself in an audio book on Amazon's Audible can be quite delicious.

Of course, you could just read a book on your phone/tablet or on your Kindle.

- **Radio**

And don't underestimate the joy of simple radio. When I have been camping by myself I have listened to morning radio on the car stereo system but it is not the best way to listen and could annoy the neighbours so it is worth investing in a proper radio for the back of the van. It's quite useful to have one that can be hung up somewhere so that it is out of the way.

You can buy compact, portable DAB/FM radios that run on the mains or on batteries so that it is easy to move it around the van or play if you are not on hook-up. Some also have a socket for headphones so that one person can listen to the radio if the other is reading or sleeping.

You can, of course, receive radio via your phone/tablet/laptop by downloading the station's app. When Chris Evans moved from BBC Radio 2 to Virgin radio I was dismayed as I really enjoy listening to him in the mornings. However, it was really easy (and free) to download the Virgin radio app on my tablet and then sync it by Bluetooth to a mini speaker that I can move around the house.

Whatever kit you use to entertain yourselves, if it is an electronic arrangement it is best to try it out at home before you come away so that you can get used to it and iron out any glitches or incompatibilities.

Non-Electronic Entertainment (Yes it does exist!)

Let's not forget good old-fashioned board games. With board games you will need to find somewhere to store them but, if you are a family, it may well be worth it for those wet days and evenings. Check out a new book (at 2019) that will give you ideas for some tabletop games you may not have even heard of before - *"The Everything Tabletop Games Book: From Settlers of Catan to Pandemic, Find Out Which Games to Choose, How to Play, and the Best Ways to Win!"* by Bebo on Amazon.

And, of course, there are always plenty of card games to play and you only need to store a small pack of cards which you can take with you to a café and play on a wet morning too. This takes me back to the time when I backpacked around India for a month with three friends and we took a cribbage board and cards with us. In two teams of two we played an on-going tournament of cribbage throughout the trip which we called 'The Bombay-to-Bombay Run' and it was a great way to spend the time when we were waiting for transport which, in India, could take hours.

19. The Feng Shui of Campervans

Now, I realise that this subject may not be for everybody so, if it's not for you, then please just skip this chapter. However, if you are even just the tiniest bit intrigued, let me tell you about the Feng Shui of campervans.

Every space has its own particular Feng Shui. Feng Shui (pronounced '*fong shway*') is an ancient Chinese art that says that the way your house is built or the way that you arrange objects affects your success, health, and happiness. It can be applied to your desk at work through to the town you are living in, but mostly Feng Shui is associated with buildings *(see the end of this chapter for a fuller explanation of the art of Feng Shui)*. These buildings may be your home, your office or your temple and, to me, our campervans are our homes on wheels so they too will have their own kind of Feng Shui.

The Feng Shui of a house is affected by, not only what is inside it, but also the land underneath it. The main difference between a campervan and a house is that the campervan moves around so is influenced by the energy of many different pieces of ground, whereas a house it fixed so will be profoundly affected by the land underneath it, for better or worse. If our house is built on 'sick' land, say you have underground water flowing there, fault lines or radon in the ground (like many places in Cornwall do), then your house could become a 'sick building' and you may find that you struggle with your health while you are there. This is known as geophysical stress.

Geo-psychic Stress

Properties can also suffer from Geo-psychic stress where strong emotional events get stuck in that place and overlay the healthy energy blueprint of that land. When I was a Feng Shui consultant I was called to several houses that were built over or near old battlefield sites and the occupants were experiencing a lot of family difficulty there as they were affected by the stuck imprint of conflict in that land.

Some homes even have what I call a 'House Script' in the land beneath them. This is when there is an invisible drama that keeps repeating in that building, attracting the same type of people and events to it - same play, different actors. I've come across divorce houses, wealth houses, poverty houses, male or female-only houses, fertility houses, career houses, accident houses and all sorts.

Of course, in a campervan, you will be parked over all different types of 'scripts' so they won't have much influence on your life or relationships, especially as you are only likely to be there for a short time. However, more and more people are now living in their campervans so this factor will become more important if you are doing that.

Being sensitive to such things, there have been times when we have been parked just overnight in the van where I have had a very disturbed night because of the vibes there. We have also stayed at some magical places that have the most gorgeous energy and one of my favourite places like this is our wild spot in a wood on Dartmoor in Devon. While I am there, I almost feel like I am in a scene of from the film, Avatar, where the forest lights up as you walk by!

If you are a sensitive person too, and I expect more of you are than you know (especially the children), then you might have had similar experiences yourself. If you haven't, I encourage you to try and feel the energy of the place that you are staying in, especially if you are going wild, as it can be quite fun to do this.

Anyway, for a campervan, the land beneath you will be constantly changing so let's look at the Feng Shui of the interior of a campervan. (NOTE: there is NO judgement about what you choose to have in your van or house space, just whether it is right *for you* and your co-travellers at this point in time.)

What to Look for in the interior of your van

There are many things in a room/van interior that affect your mood as well as affect you on a practical level:

- The Bagua Template
- Flow of Movement
- Colours
- Safety

- **The Bagua Template**

Anything that you own tells a story about you whether it's your bookshelf, your phone, your clothes or your campervan. Whatever we have in our lives, especially our home, has been consciously or unconsciously chosen by us and so has to be an expression of who we are and the life we are living.

In Feng Shui, what objects/furniture you chose to have in your space and where you place them in your house (or a room) will tell a story about different parts of your life.

Specific areas in the house will relate to: your wealth, your relationships, your health, your community, your spirituality, your career and it is possible to read a person's life by walking around their house if you know what to look for. Many years ago when I was dating, I would always quietly check the Feng Shui of my potential partner's home and there were times that I exited that liaison because of what I read from his home. The Feng Shui never lies!

Another example was one of my Feng Shui clients. She was an attractive and successful young woman who wanted to find a partner relationship but was having difficulty for no apparent reason. When I looked around her house, there were lots of objects, pictures and general layout that really talked about the single life which she had been enjoying up until now. In the relationship area of her bedroom (the most important relationship area in a house, there was even a picture of a quote (which I can't remember now) but it was along the lines of "stay free and single"! (Interestingly, the career and wealth areas of her house were very strong, so it was no surprise that she had a very lucrative career in the media).

Although she had shifted emotionally inside herself and was wanting to go into a new phase in her life, her home was telling a different story. We talked about this and it came out that, although she wanted to have a life partner now, there was a part of her that was a little scared and was a little resistant to giving up the advantages of a single life and her home as reflecting this. As she talked about her concerns and let them see the light of day, it enabled her to process these now unhelpful, unconscious programs and make space for something new to happen.

I encouraged her to start putting objects around the house in pairs and select new pictures/quotes that had a more romantic feel to them and generally set the stage in her home as it there were two people living there. (it didn't matter if her and her new partner were going to live there or not, by setting the stage in your space you are creating the blueprint in your life for the new 'play').

It wasn't long before she found her Mr Right and, as far as I know, they had a long and happy relationship. This is the power of The Bagua - or the template within your house, room or van.

The Bagua in a Nutshell

The Bagua template is a bit like a grid that lines up with the entrance of the room/house/van. It is sort of like a fractal in that it is the same in the tiniest space, like a desk, or in a large area, like a town. It is a universal principle that applies wherever you are.

If this is all a bit too woo woo for you just take away from this that it is good to be conscious of what you put in your personal living/camping spaces and make it a positive choice rather than something unconscious or random. On a basic biological level we are affected by our environment in subtle ways so make sure that what you see and feel around you makes you feel happy and is in line with who you are now or who you want to be in the future.

- **Flow of Movement**

Unlike a house, your campervan has a split personality; it has its day mode and its night mode, and it can feel like a completely different space depending on what mode it is in. To get the best flow in a van you need to think of each mode differently and consider what the job is of each configuration as what we need from night mode is very different from what we need from day mode.

Van in Day Mode: The sort of things we need our space to provide for us in day mode is:

- somewhere to sit
- somewhere to eat
- somewhere to cook
- somewhere to store food
- somewhere to store clothes
- somewhere to shelter from weather
- somewhere to work on a computer (for some people)
- somewhere to go to the loo (for some vans)
- somewhere to wash/shower (for some vans)
- somewhere to play board games/computer games

This is a lot to ask of a small space that may only be a few square metres. So, you might want to think about how your van will flow from say, cooking/eating function to playing function. How easy is it to flow in and out of your storage? How easy is it to flow from inside the van to outside the van if you want to cook/sit outside for a while? How easy is it to flow from storage function (clothes) to wash/shower function? What is the flow pattern if different people want to do different things at the same time?

Van in Night Mode: The sort of things we need our campervan to provide for us in night mode is:

- somewhere to sleep
- somewhere to watch TV/relax
- Somewhere to pee (maybe)
- Somewhere for passion

Of course, it is unlikely that any small van will be able to do all these things perfectly so some compromise will be needed but it is good to know what you can compromise on and what you really don't want to compromise on before you buy/convert your van.

- **Colours**

Colours have a huge effect on our mood and how much we enjoy a space. For example, being in a red room can raise your heartrate and a blue or green room will make you feel calm and at ease. Colours like orange and yellow are energising and optimistic and white makes you feel that a space is clean. Black is a heavier colour and just imagine how you would feel if you were in a room that was all black. Pink is about gentleness and love and they have found that, by painting the walls in a prison a light pink, the inmates were much calmer and their general behaviour radically improved. However, everyone is different and how we respond to different colours can change throughout our lives and what we need at the time.

On a more practical level, colour can drastically affect the visual of a space and make it feel darker/lighter, bigger/smaller, cleaner/messier. Generally lighter colours make a space feel bigger and this is something to bear in mind in your campervan. However, if you want to feel like you are in a cosy nest then darker, warmer colours would work well.

And then there is the effect created when different colours are put together and how comfortable or uncomfortable that combination feels. This is a huge subject and if you want to explore it further just Google 'The Colour Wheel' and you will see the sort of colour palettes that work well.

- **How Safe Does it Feel?**

Although we now live in a digital world, on a biological level we are still just mammals. This means that we are still governed by our basic survival instincts even if we do overlay them with social niceties (well, some of us). This means that, on an unconscious level we are still monitoring and checking our environment all the time for safety. One of the classic No-Nos in Feng Shui is sitting with your back to the door, especially if it is somewhere where you sit a lot like your desk. On a hormonal, neuropeptide level we will be unable to fully relax as our animal part feels it must stay alert for any intruders/attackers coming through the door.

Another thing in our environment that will make us feel on edge is sharp edges. If you have sharp corners or edges pointing at you, especially where you are sleeping or sitting, this can make you feel uncomfortable as though invisible daggers are coming at you.

And then there are safety factors on the practical level like: can I find the key easily if I need to drive away fast, is the gas safe and secure, is there anything stored above that might fall on my head, am I going to bump into things that might injure me? Of course, you may not be conscious of these things, but your inner mammal is and will not rest until he/she feels safe.

> ***What is Feng Shui?***
>
> *Feng Shui is an ancient art and science that was formalized over 3,000 years ago in China. In literal translation feng means "wind" and shui means "water." In Chinese culture, wind and water are associated with good health, thus good Feng Shui*

came to mean good fortune. Conversely, bad Feng Shui means bad luck or misfortune.

Some elements of Feng Shui practice date back at least 6,000 years, and it contains elements of various branches of scholarly study, including physics, philosophy, astronomy, and astrology. It is related closely to the Taoist vision and understanding of nature, particularly the idea that the land is alive and filled with chi or energy.

Feng Shui is sometimes thought to be the art of placement—understanding how the placement of yourself and objects within a space affects your life in various areas of experience. It is a complex body of knowledge that teaches you how to balance and harmonize with the energies in any given space—be it a home, office, or garden. Its aim is to assure good fortune for the people inhabiting a space. Although regarded by some in the scientific community as a pseudo-science, Feng Shui has had an impact on the aesthetics of interior design and the architectural layout of living and working spaces both in its native eastern and, more recently, western cultures.

Since good fortune comes in many forms, including better health, a successful career, or fulfilling love life, Feng Shui practice includes detailed tips for almost every area of your life. The main tools used in analysing the Feng Shui of any space are the Feng Shui compass and the Bagua.

From www.thespruce.com

About the Author
Summer Bourne

Summer Bourne writes a campervan-foodie blog that celebrates the campervan life and shares easy camping recipes on her blog and in her books.

Summer and her partner, Glyn, were tent-campers for many years but got fed up with putting up a tent in the half-light on a Friday night or taking it down in the rain at the end of a wet weekend so decided to buy themselves a small campervan. They went to the campervan shows but realised that their very small budget would buy them barely more than a wheel there! But then they found a company that sold converted Toyota Previas for a reasonable price and their first campervan, 'Trev-the-Prev' came into their life.

As time went on, they decided that they needed a bigger van and that they would design it themselves as, by then, they knew what they wanted and what they didn't want in their campervan. So, they bought a red SWB Vauxhall Vivaro crew van ('Big Red') and converted it into the campervan that really works for them.

Summer spent many hundreds of hours researching vans and interiors in campervans and admits that she became slightly obsessed with it and now describes herself as a van geek. She is also a member of the South Central Self-Build Get Together club which meets in the New Forest throughout the summer to convert their vans together, barbeque and chat about all things campervan.

As part of her campervan journey, Summer has become passionate about camping cooking and having easy, tasty and nutritious food while you are on the road. She has written a cookbook 'The Camper Cookie' and a book about her campervan life called 'Adventures of a Lazy Campervan Cook'.

In her former life she has been an engineer, technical copywriter, accounts technician, Feng Shui consultant, business owner and author.

To check out Summer's blog go to:
www.thecampercookie.com

One Last Thing...

If you have enjoyed this book or found it useful, I'd be very grateful if you would post a review on Amazon. Your support really does make a difference and I read all the reviews personally so that I can get your feedback and hopefully make my books even better.

Thank you for your support!

Printed in Great Britain
by Amazon

71035475R00078